AUTHOR'S INTRODUCTION

Welcome to the wonderful world of newt-keeping. You have excellent taste in pets, my friend—I have been charmed by newts for many, many years, and, hopefully, so have you. If not, then I must warn you—it's a tough road to steer away from once you've started down it. Newts are marvelous creatures, but you'll find that out soon enough.

In this handy little book, you will be introduced to many facets of newt-keeping; housing, feeding, breeding, etc. In an early chapter I'm even going to go over some natural history aspects concerning a few of our little friends. I'm not going to claim that any of that information will improve your keeping skills, but it may enhance your knowledge of newts and thus further your own intrigue. Beyond the text, you will also find a seemingly endless supply of beautiful full-color illustrations, all of which will pique your appreciation for what is perhaps the most enjoyable aspect of the newts—their visual appeal. By the time you've finished with the book, you'll be something of an expert in your own right.

I hope you enjoy every word.

Jordan Patterson
April, 1994

MICHAEL GILROY

One of the most popular members of the family Salamandridae, the Fire Salamander, *Salamandra salamandra*, has been bred many times in captivity.

DEDICATION

And this one I dedicate to John Quinn and Alex Young. Gentlemen, it is a privilege to walk upon the same earth as you.

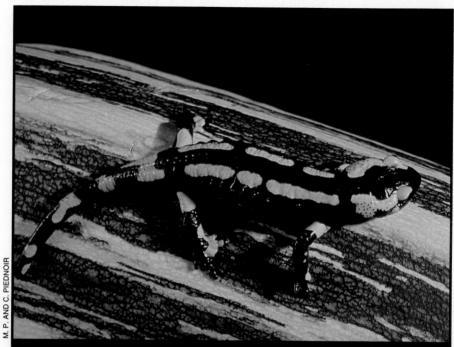

M. P. AND C. PIEDNOIR

The Fire Salamander, *Salamandra salamandra*, can be found in parts of Africa, Europe, and Asia. It is a hardy captive, taking a variety of livefoods, often right from a keeper's fingers.

NATURAL HISTORY

In this chapter, I'm going to discuss a little natural history concerning each of the seven genera of newts that this book is focused on. In the family Salamandridae, to which all the newts belong, there is an actual total of 15 genera. The reason I chose only the seven that I did was because those are the ones that seem to be most often kept in captivity and therefore the ones that 99 % of the readers will be most interested in and able to relate to.

THE FAMILY SALAMANDRIDAE

As I said a moment ago, all the amphibians we call the "newts" in English are placed in the family Salamandridae. They are found primarily in a geographic zone called the Holearctic Region, which comprises almost all of the Northern Hemisphere and is broken into two main sectors—the Palearctic (Old World) and the Nearctic (New World). There are salamandridids in both eastern and western North America, Europe, and in central and

The Red-spotted Newt, *Notophthalmus viridescens viridescens*, is commonly seen in the herpetocultural hobby. It is native to much of the eastern half of the United States.

W. P. MARA

eastern Asia. The most genera occur in Europe—nine—then there are six in Asia, and only two in North America. The fifteen genera are as follows:

Chioglossa——Gold-striped Salamanders

Cynops——Fire-bellied Newts

Euproctus——Brook Salamanders

Mertensiella——Spine-tailed Salamanders

Neurergus——Near Eastern Newts

Notophthalmus——Eastern Newts

Pachytriton——Small-eyed Newts

Paramesotriton——Warty Newts

Pleurodeles——Ribbed Newts

Salamandra——Fire Salamanders

Salamandrina——Italian Four-toed Salamanders

Taricha——Western Newts

Triturus——European Newts

Tylototriton——Crocodile Newts

Most salamandridids do not grow over a total body length of 8 in/20 cm, but a few, those in either *Pleurodeles* or *Salamandra*, can reach up to 14 in/35 cm. The skin of a salamandridid is usually fairly granular because their bodies are covered with poison glands. The poisons from these glands are the most toxic of any salamander. Thus, relative to so many other poisonous amphibians, most salamandridids are quite strikingly colored, this of course being a constant warning to any would-be predators.

A primarily aquatic group, newts of the genus *Cynops* often have dark-colored dorsums (backs), and, in contrast, the bellies are usually very bright, in yellows, reds, or oranges.

W. P. MARA

W. P. MARA

Above: Note the strong dorsal ridge and the rough skin on this Hong Kong Warty Newt, *Paramesotriton hongkongensis*.
Below: The Warty Newts, genus *Paramesotriton*, are native primarily to Asia and can be found in cool, flowing waters. They make excellent captives and are often seen in the pet trade.

W. P. MARA

As for reproduction, most salamandridids lay eggs in water, although the exceptions are the few that lay theirs on land and two species that give live birth (*Salamandra atra* and *Mertensiella luschani*). In all cases of egglayers, the larvae are aquatic and have a free-living stage, but then, depending on the genera, they can branch into three different life cycles. In one, the larvae metamorphose and remain aquatic all throughout their lives. In another, the larvae transform and then live life on land, only returning to the water in order to breed. Finally, there are those that go from water as larvae into a terrestrial stage as juveniles (known as an "eft" stage), and then return to aquatic life as adults.

SEVEN GENERA OF NEWTS— *CYNOPS, NOTOPHTHALMUS, PARAMESOTRITON, PLEURODELES, TARICHA, TRITURUS,* AND *TYLOTOTRITON*

Cynops—Fire-bellied Newts

Found in the southern Palearctic Region, the Fire-bellied Newts were first described by Tschudi in 1839. Only four or five species are recognized although there is thought to be about eight different forms altogether (the rest

Found in China and Japan, the Fire-bellied Newts, genus *Cynops*, are not only easy to keep, but can be, and have been, bred in captivity with little effort on the keeper's part.

R. D. BARTLETT

R. T. ZAPPALORTI

This "ref eft" is representative of the terrestrial stage of the Red-spotted Newt, *Notophthalmus viridescens*. The eft stage is the second of three stages in their life cycle. During the third, they return to the water to breed, and then remain aquatic from then on.

are considered subspecies). *Cynops* is generally considered a close relative of the Western Newts, genus *Taricha.* Fire-bellied Newts lack the dorsal crest that is seen on so many other newts, and they have a laterally flattened tail that often tapers off into what appears to be a thin thread. They are basically darkly colored animals, usually a very dark brown, gray, or even black, with bright bellies, usually yellow, reddish, or orange, that are often spotted or mottled with the same dark dorsal coloring. They are mostly aquatic and can be found in still waters that are either quite cool or fairly warm depending on the locality of the population.

Notophthalmus—Eastern Newts

Among the most visually attractive of all newts, the Eastern Newts were first described by Rafinesque in 1820. They are found primarily in the United States, but then run southward into northeastern Mexico. *Notophthalmus* has been compared to *Triturus* in many respects. The hind legs are generally much more powerful than the front, and during the breeding season the males show off their black nuptial pads. There is no prominent dorsal crest per se, but in some specimens a vague dorsal ridge is visible. Most, however, appear basically tubular. The base color is usually brown or a dark and pale greenish, with red, orange, and black spots. The bellies are also yellow or orange, and covered with more tiny black spots; most specimens are deceptively attractive. There are somewhere around four species; one, the Red-spotted Newt, *Nothophalmus viridescens viridescens*, being one of the most popular pet newts in the United States.

The life cycle of the Eastern Newts is really rather fascinating. Mating begins in either the spring or autumn, in shallow pools and ponds. The males grab the females from above, either around the chest or the neck, and will hover above them for what could be up to a few hours, then will suddenly drop a spermatophore and leave moment later. The females lay their eggs in the spring, and the clutch count is somewhere around 250. The larvae only need about three or four weeks to hatch, and then metamorphose no more than 12 or 13 weeks later. Some specimens remain more or less in larval form throughout their lives and never really leave the water. Most, however, become terrestrial for up to three years, and this phase of their life is called their "eft" stage. If you ever get the chance to see one of these efts (usually referred to with a modifier—red eft), take it—they are very, very beautiful. As they leave their eft stage, becoming sexually mature, they return to the water, become aquatic once again, and remain that way for the rest of their lives. There have

been many reports of literally hundreds of red efts migrating across roads on their way to breeding ponds during cool spring nights as they head toward their final life cycle destination.

***Paramesotriton*—Warty Newts**

(See photos on page 5.) Found primarily in China and North Vietnam, the Warty Newts have been quite popular with hobbyists in recent years. They get their common name from the very rough texture of their skin. There are about a half dozen accepted species, and can be found in cool, flowing waters. They have long, laterally flattened tails and no dorsal crest. Most species are unspectacularly colored until you get to the belly, which can be very striking and which these newts will show off when they feel threatened. A reasonably young genus, first

One of the rarer *Notophthalmus* subspecies, the Broken-striped Newt, *Notophthalmus viridescens dorsalis*, is native only to the Coastal Plains of North and South Carolina. Photo: K. T. Nemuras.

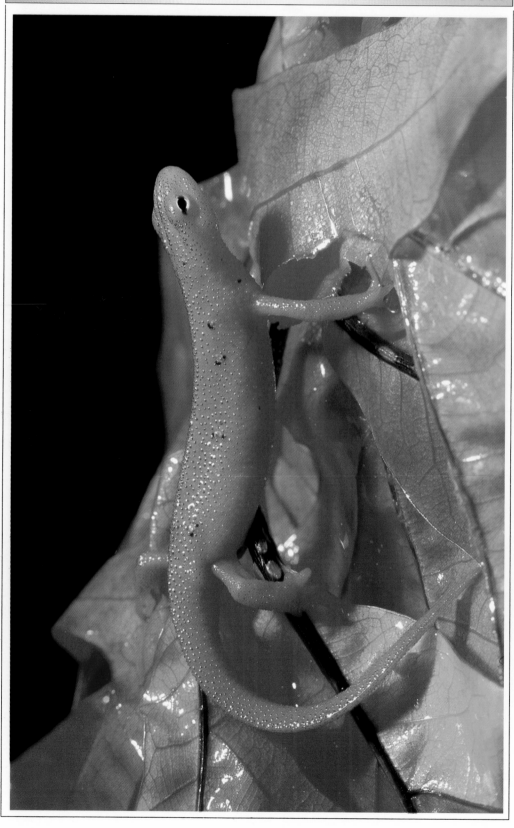

being described by Chang in 1935. Not a lot is known about their mating behavior except it is believed to be quite similar to that of *Triturus*. Wild specimens breed during the cooler seasons.

Pleurodeles—Ribbed Newts

Occurring primarily in the southwestern Palearctic Region, the Ribbed Newts were first described by Michahelles in 1830. There are only two species, *P. poireti*, the Algerian Ribbed Newt, and *P. waltl*, the Spanish Ribbed Newt, but only *waltl* is ever seen in captivity. They can grow up to 12 in/30 cm, which is fairly respectable for a newt, and can be found in fairly warm, vegetated, and standing water. Their tails are long, laterally compressed, and pointed, and their bodies are somewhat stout. On the lateral region one may notice a row of soft points; these are made by the ribs. In fact, most interestingly, in some *P. waltl*, the ribs actually pop through the skin, apparently causing no harm, or even discomfort, to the animal whatsoever. The larvae of this genus are fairly elongated. Also, during the breeding season, the males, whose tails are longer than the females's, will boast black nuptial pads, visible inside the arms and on the hands.

Facing Page: Red efts are, like most other newts, relatively easy to keep in captivity. If you can acquire a steady supply of small vertebrates and invertebrates (earthworms, crickets, etc.), then you should have no problems maintaining them. Photo: K. T. Nemuras.

The Ribbed Newts are apparently very active, fairly aggressive creatures, but most keepers might not notice—they are largely active during the early morning or early evening hours. The rest of the time, particular during the day, they hide themselves, so it is important that a keeper give them someplace where they can feel obscured (if not, they will become quite stressed). They are more or less completely aquatic, although one small body of land will be necessary in a tank setup. In the wild, *Pleurodeles* has no specific breeding season, so getting them to breed in captivity is largely a matter of trickery and know-how. The males, when ready, will swim under the females and rub their throats with their heads. Then they will grasp the females front legs and, eventually, release a spermatophore near the female's mouth. Afterward, the males will turn the females around so the spermatophore can be collected. Up to nearly 1000 eggs have been laid from a single female, but this is unusual. The normal number is somewhere around 400 to 600. The eggs are usually laid in clumps and adhere to whatever object happens to be nearby.

Taricha—Western Newts

First described by Gray in 1850, the Western Newts are the only other newt genus aside from *Notophthalmus* to be found in the United States. Their general range begins in southern Alaska along the Pacific Coast, all the way down to northern Baja California.

DAVID GREEN

Among the most long-lived of all the newts are those in the genus *Taricha*. Specimens over fifteen years old are not unknown, and sexual maturity is not reached until after the fifth.

There are only three species at present, all of which appear in the hobby from time to time (the California Newt, *Taricha torosa*, is undoubtedly the most popular). They are well built and grow to about 8 in/20 cm. The eyes are large and well offset from the head, being an attractive light coppery color. Virtually all specimens have a simple two-toned coloration—brown on the back, and yellow or orange on the belly. The line where these two colors meet can be easily seen on the laterum. Their skin is fairly rough and there is no prominent dorsal crest, but toward the tail a faint ridge becomes apparent. Males become quite smooth-skinned during the breeding season and boast their nuptial pads on their hands and feet.

Interestingly, *Taricha* newts are remarkably long-lived, which can be ascertained from the fact that sexual maturity is not reached by at least the fifth year of life. Also, these newts seem to have a most acute homing instinct, returning to the same ponds and pools to breed, During these breeds, the females will be greatly outnumbered, for it is generally believed that females are only biannual breeders at best, some

Facing Page: Discovered in southern Spain in the early 1800's, the Spanish Ribbed Newt, *Pleurodeles waltl*, grows to about 30 cm, making it the largest of all European newts. Photo: Paul Freed.

KEN LUCAS

The Rough-skinned Newt, *Taricha granulosa*, can be distinguished from its brother the California Newt, *Taricha torosa*, by its dark lower eyelid. In *torosa*, the lower eyelid is considerably lighter.

during breeding season. The males become much more brilliantly colored during this time and have a very conspicuous crest. There are somewhere around nine species, plus a whole load of subspecies (somewhere in the neighborhood of three dozen). Breeding takes place immediately following winter dormancy and the female can lay hundreds of eggs over a period of a few months. Larvae will hatch in about two or three weeks and transform only a few months later. Outside of the breeding season, *Triturus* is more or less terrestrial. Most species have been bred in captivity at least a few times.

Tylototriton–Crocodile Newts

Found in China, northern Southeast Asia, and parts of Japan, these fascinating animals have been growing steadily more popular in the amphibiocultural hobby. First described by Anderson in 1871, there are currently six accepted species, found in damp mountain regions at very high elevations. Interestingly, this genus used to occur in Europe as well, according to the fossil record. Their skin is

going three or even four years between breeds. The males attach themselves to the backs of the females to release the spermatophores as close to the cloacas as possible. The eggs can be deposited either singly or in clumps, depending on the species, and are usually left on the substrate. After breeding, the females return to the land whereas the males will remain in the water for awhile. Metamorphosed larvae can each a length of up to 3 in/7.5 cm.

Triturus–European Newts

The genus *Triturus* was described by Rafinesque in 1815. The European Newts are found most predominantly in the Western Palearctic, then south to Isreal, then east toward the Caspian Sea. They do not grow over 6.4 in/16 cm and have tails that change in shape, being round on land but more compressed

L. WISCHNATH

The Alpine Newt, *Triturus alpestris*, can be kept fully aquatic during all parts of the year as long as the water level in their tank is kept low during the summer months.

MELLA PANZELLA

The neatly arranged rows of "warts" and the prominent dorsal stripe are distinct characteristics of the Emperor Newt, *Tylototriton verrucosus.*

Facing Page: The Emperor Newt, *Tylototriton verrucosus,* has become very popular with herpetoculturists over the last few years. Their captive requirements are minimal and they are apparently easy to captive-breed. Photo: Jim Merli.

very rough and covered with neatly arranged, conspicuous warts. Many species look like other species and are thus difficult to tell apart purely on sight. They are fairly toxic animals as well, so wash your hands after any contact with them. They have fairly long and powerful legs, and their heads appear triangular. They are also fairly good-sized, the largest specimens growing to around 6.4 in/16 cm.

Crocodile newts spend almost all of their time on the ground and appear to be quite secretive, only coming out during the night hours to hunt for whatever tiny creatures are unfortunate enough to wander in front of them. The reproductive period apparently lasts a fairly long time for newts—over a period of months—and the eggs are somewhat large—up to 10 mm. They breed during monsoon seasons and remain somewhat inactive the rest of the time.

HOUSING NEWTS

The housing of newts has never been a particularly difficult affair. In regard to the genera we are discussing within this book, the only setups you really need are either a good-sized paludarium with a fairly large water body, or a damp terrarium that still contains, at least, a large water dish that is easily accessible to the inmates. Even climate control is not a problem, since most species don't have to be heated all that much, and those that do need very little.

gallon, for ten to 12, a 30-gallon, and for any more than that, a 55-gallon is what you'll need. Remember, many of them like to swim and will appreciate the space.

The only style of enclosure you should even consider is the glass aquarium. These of course are the ones used in fish-keeping and, for that matter, just about every other facet of herpetoculture beyond newt-keeping. I point this seemingly obvious fact out because a lot of keepers of reptiles

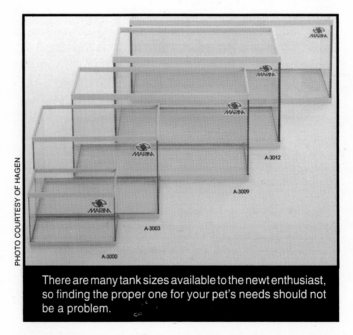

PHOTO COURTESY OF HAGEN

There are many tank sizes available to the newt enthusiast, so finding the proper one for your pet's needs should not be a problem.

SIZE AND TYPE OF TANK

First thing to think about when setting up a newt's home is how many specimens you're planning on keeping. If the answer is many, then you'll need a fairly good-sized tank. For up to three specimens, a 10-gallon tank is acceptable, for four to eight, a 20-

and amphibians enjoy building their own tanks, but, in the case of the highly aquatic newts, this really isn't very practical. There are other enclosures you could try, but in every aspect of newt-keeping there are considerations that involve, at the very least, a high level of moisture. Since glass aquariums were designed for aquatic purposes, it seems foolish to divert from them. Remember also, that tanks need security, so a sensible tank top will also need to be purchased. Newts, like any other herptiles, will gladly wander off if given the chance. Those that are totally aquatic probably won't be jumping out of the tank all that often, but a good tank top will stop foreign objects from getting in. Example—a piece of plaster or a chip of paint falls into the water and one of your newts decides to eat it. Guess what might happen next? Don't run the risk; get a tank top.

is almost standard when it comes to aquatic setups.

Gravel can be purchased at just about any pet store on earth and is reasonably cheap. It also comes in a wide variety of attractive colors and, perhaps best of all, it is reusable. The only downside to gravel is the fact that it is quite heavy to work with and may cause a few back pains during cleaning time.

In the case of terrarium setups, gravel is also acceptable, but not as practical as potting soil. Soil is not only inexpensive and can be bought in quantity at any number of places, but it also allows you to

PHOTO COURTESY OF HAGEN

Tank security is usually not a major concern with the newts, so a lighted hood like the one shown can be utilized without further worry.

CAGE IMPLEMENTS

The Substrate

In most other aspects of herptile keeping, the issue of which substrate is the best is always under scrutiny, but in the case of aquatic newts, I think the answer is rather obvious—gravel is truly the best choice. As many keepers are already aware, gravel

include live plants into the setup, which terrestrial newts certainly will have no objection to.

Live Plants

I think it really is a must for any newt-keeper to include a few plants into his or her setup, whether that setup be terrestrial or aquatic. Many aquatic newt species naturally live in areas where their waters are literally plant-choked. Aquatic plants not only are attractive and inexpensive, but they do that much more to create a realistic home for your newts. Aquatic plants of many types can be purchased at pet stores that sell fish, and you can inquire with the dealer as to which ones work best with newts. Terrestrial plants can be purchased at most any garden or home-improvement center and most are so inexpensive that the prices are almost negligible.

A quick note on artificial plants—these are perfectly usable with newts, both aquatic and terrestrial, but are not advisable in a breeding tank. Beyond that, they can be used whenever and wherever the keeper's feels they should be used.

Large Rocks

For the purpose of creating land areas in aquatic setups, there's nothing easier than large rocks. Large rocks are not only reusable and fairly easy to work with (after all, they shouldn't be *too* large), but they can be easily obtained—either in nature, from a garden store, from a landscaper's supply house, or from a pet store. Be careful, of course, when placing them in a glass aquarium. I say this because I, occasional idiot that I am, have dropped a large rock or two not into but *through* glass tanks that I was setting up for newts. One way to create some good-sized land bodies out of rocks is by situating a few large

Artificial plants can be used with aquatic setups and are just as safe as real plants. Another benefit of artificial plants is that they can be cleaned and re-used indefinitely.

PHOTO COURTESY OF TETRA/SECOND NATURE

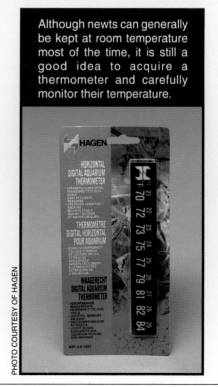

Although newts can generally be kept at room temperature most of the time, it is still a good idea to acquire a thermometer and carefully monitor their temperature.

PHOTO COURTESY OF HAGEN

rocks so they just barely break the water's surface, then place one large and very flat rock across all the others.

In terrestrial setups, rocks will create welcome hiding places for your newts, many of which will burrow right under them. If you are careful enough, you can even build little caves for your pets. Again, flat rocks are better for terrarium setups than round or otherwise bulky ones.

CLIMATE CONTROL

Heating

Perhaps the most convenient part of newt-keeping is the fact that virtually all species can be kept at room temperature, and some, in fact, even a little cooler than that. In short, this means no heating apparatus is necessary.

The ideal ambient temperature for newts is around 60 to 65°F/16 to 18°C. When breeding season rolls around (in the spring), you will have to raise the temperature a little bit, which can be done naturally if you live in an area where the seasons are well-defined. Otherwise, you can do this through the use of a submersible heater.

Lighting

Newts, unlike turtles and lizards, are not in crucial need of something called "full-spectrum lighting," (which, in short, is lighting that replicates the light given off by the sun), but instead can survive just fine with ordinary light.

You can supply such lighting a number of ways. One is to park the setup near a window and let the sun do it for you. Since newt tanks don't need to be overtly warmed or specially lit, this is the method I have always chosen. Since I live in what is known as a temperate zone, the changing of seasons is very obvious. This is very important when

For certain newt species, a slight warming of their water body may be necessary. When this is the case, fully submersible heaters are probably best.

PHOTO COURTESY OF HAGEN

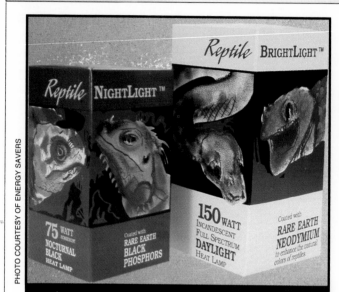

PHOTO COURTESY OF ENERGY SAVERS

There are a number of products currently being produced that will effectively help you replicate the correct day-night cycle (photoperiod) for your newts.

summer.

An easy way to assure this without having to go to too much trouble is to simply hook your lighting apparatus up to a timer. The timer settings can be changed as the weeks pass, accurately replicating the photoperiod in each of the seasons.

Humidity

In tanks that contain terrestrial newts that live in warmer regions, one simple way to provide humidity and moisture is to place a sheet of clear-plastic food wrap over the top of the tank, poking a few tiny holes in it so some air can get through. In no time at all the water will start condensing on the sides of the glass. You can maintain this humidity and the ensuing moisture by peeling the plastic wrap back every five days and gently misting everything with a spray bottle. Soil will of course hold the moisture very well, and the further addition of the plastic wrap will keep the rising moisture in the tank. Even in a relatively cool room, a setup of this sort will remain fairly warm and humid.

Ventilation

Since newts are so cold-adaptable, and since fresh air is a very important provision for captive herptiles, it is advised that

bringing newts into breeding condition, but we will get to that later.

The other method is through the use of artificial light. Whether you choose a regular household light bulb or a fluorescent, it really doesn't make a difference. The newts won't care either way.

The issue of photoperiod is very important with newts. In short, photoperiod is the amount of time light is exposed to something (in this case, the newts). The ideal photoperiod for newts will vary from season to season, but, as I mentioned above, it is very important for telling them when breeding season has begun. In general a newt should not be given any light during the winter (as it will be hibernating during this time), about six to eight hours per day in the spring and fall, then gradually leading up to around ten to twelve in the

PHOTO COURTESY OF RIVER TANK

Rather than go to the time and trouble of setting up a tank from scratch, many keepers might want to consider buying a pre-made paludarium.

plastic wrap discussed a moment ago, ventilation will be provided when the keeper peels the wrap back every few days to mist-spray.

FILTRATION

The issue of filtration in regard to *any* aquatic herptile has always been a hot one, especially with regard to aquatic turtles (which are, without a doubt, among the filthiest creatures that ever moved upon this earth).

But with newts, the filtration issue really isn't as alarming. They aren't, in truth, all that messy, and thus there is no reason why a good, sensible filtration setup wouldn't keep their tank perfectly sanitary. There are a number of different types of filters available to the keeper of highly aquatic newts, but the two most sensible and practical styles are the box filter and the undergravel filter. Either of these can be purchased at your local pet

you allow as much air to flow freely through a newt's tank as possible while, of course, still affording adequate tank security and making sure there aren't any blatantly cold drafts blowing around. Satisfactory ventilation can be provided by simply making sure there are openings in the tank lid. In the case of using the

There are a handful of different filter styles that can be used with aquatic newts. Those of the under-gravel type are very effective and can be purchased in most any pet shop.

PHOTO COURTESY OF HAGEN

PHOTO COURTESY OF HAGEN

The AquaClear Power Head filters are used extensively in the fish-keeping hobby and can be used with newts as well. There are a number of different styles available.

store, along with their respective components (filter floss, charcoal, tubing, etc.) and are usually quite inexpensive.

The necessity of having a filter is obvious—it keeps the water clean and thus keeps the newts in good health. Beyond that, filters keep the keeper from having to change the water every three days. Filters are, for these and many other reasons, greatly helpful in newt-keeping. Use them.

TANK CLEANING

This subheading really should be included in a chapter on diseases and so forth because cage cleaning is, without question, an affair that is directly related to disease prevention (all good husbandry techniques are, but this one is massively

important). The truth is, many captive reptiles and amphibians fall victim to disease because their keepers don't practice the cage-cleaning ritual as often as they should or as efficiently as they should.

I will offer a simple step-by-step cage-cleaning method that has been utilized by a number of keepers, including myself, throughout the years, with great success. You can follow it to the letter or modify it here and there to suit your needs, but it is most important that you *do* keep your pets's tanks clean, because prevention of diseases is a great deal easier than curing them.

1) Remove all the newts and put them in a secure container. This can be nearly anything suitable, i.e., a plastic shoebox or sweaterbox, a bucket with a

locking lid, a large jar, etc. Fill the container with a little water too.

2) Remove all climate-control items, such as lights, heating apparatus, etc.

3) Remove all items from the tank that are washable and reusable and place them in a bucket. This includes gravel, large rocks, and so forth.

4) Remove all disposable items, whatever they may be, and throw them away. This, obviously, includes filthy water.

5) Remove all plants, if there are any, and place them in suitable temporary containers.

6) Fill the now-empty tank with a mixture of warm water, dish soap, and a splash of bleach. The bleach is of course the most powerful cleanser and will effectively destroy most any germs that would otherwise threaten your newts's health. Scrub the tank clean with a plastic pad (not steel wool, for the glass will get badly scratched), paying special attention to the corners, where the glass meets the plastic rim, and other such subtle spots.

7) Empty out the warm water/soap/bleach mixture and rinse the tank very thoroughly in cold water. Keep rinsing until the effluent is clear and holds no further scent of bleach.

8) Dry the tank thoroughly.

9) Using the same method, now clean all reusable tank items.

10) Now set up the tank again and place the newts back into it.

Finally, it should be pointed out that there really isn't any need to

Some keepers choose to buy all their aquatic setup components in one convenient package, and this, really, is most sensible, not to mention economical.

PHOTO COURTESY OF HAGEN

set a concrete cleaning schedule for yourself; simply tend to the tanks whenever they get dirty.

SETTING UP THE TANK

Although you may find yourself faced with a number of tank setup choices when keeping many other types of herptiles, with newts there is really only two—the paludarium (with, again, a fairly large water body), or the terrarium.

The Paludarium Setup

The first step is getting the tank ready. Start off right—give it a good washing. It is always a good idea to begin with a clean tank.

After that, load up the gravel substrate (unless, of course, you choose to use an undergravel filter, which naturally should go in before the gravel!) Since it is more sensible to use large rocks or floating objects as land bodies, I am not going to suggest creating a land body by piling up a large amount of gravel at one end of the tank. Not only does this add unnecessary stress to the tank, but it makes the tank weigh about as much as a car, which really affords you some great fun when it comes time to clean it.

Bed the tank with about a one-inch layer of gravel, then add in your filtration system. After that has been hooked up, you can add in the water. Ordinary tap water is fine in most cases; just make sure the water in your area is not

The Marbled Newt, *Triturus marmoratus*, is a resident of Iberia and southern and western France, and can be kept in a cool terrarium setup.

M.P. AND C. PIEDNOIR

JOHN COBORN

The Spanish Ribbed Newt, *Pleurodeles waltl*, which is very popular with hobbyists, is primarily an aquatic animal and is therefore best kept in a paludarium with a very broad water body.

too alkaline or riddled with any other chemicals. There will always be a small degree of this to deal with when getting water from a faucet, so if you really want to go the total purist route, boil the water first. After it has cooled overnight, it will be safe to use.

Once the water has been added (about half the depth of the tank), carefully add in the plants (or plant the plants, you might say), and finally, put in the land bodies, whatever they may be. Turn on the filter and you're ready to go.

The Terrarium Setup

You begin, again, with a nice, freshly washed tank, then bed it with about a one–or two-inch layer of sterile potting soil (don't use soil from your own backyard because you never know what might be crawling around in it). After the soil has been added, place a few live plants in, then a couple of rocks (which, as I mentioned elsewhere, you may want to arrange in such a way as to create hiding caves). Take the time to lay out all this stuff in a manner that is attractive to your eye. Remember, the newts won't really care either way, but you're the one who'll have to look at it everyday.

The waterbowl should be quite large with a terrarium setup, because, as you know, all newts like to spend at least some time in the water. A waterbowl can be obtained at any number of places and should ideally be about eight inches in diameter (at least) and allow for about two inches of water. Place the bowl close to the rocks or plants so the newts won't have any trouble getting into it. Also, a further rock or two needs to be placed into the waterbowl itself so the newts can climb back out. Remember this, because if you don't, they very well may drown. Waterbowls don't need to be bowls, either; it's just a word I've gotten used to using over the years. You can use just about anything that meets the requirements, like a plastic shoebox for example.

Once you have all the terrarium components in place, set up any climate control items you feel are necessary, put the tank's top in place, and then let the newts go free in their new home.

"Generic Equivalent" Tank Setups

I love this phrase. "Generic Equivalent" sounds so...official, doesn't it? Almost like I'm some kind of world newt authority who spends too much time with his dictionary.

But it is a useful phrase,

regardless of how pompous it sounds. In short, it is the term for a tank setup that is dedicated to simplicity yet still completely functional for the needs at hand. And, in the case of newts, it doesn't take much.

In the case of a Paludarium Equivalent, you start off with a plastic sweaterbox or a small glass tank. Then you add in some water, then some rocks just above the level of the water but not so close to the edge of the container that the newts can wander off into your house somewhere. With the Terrarium Equivalent, you take, again, a plastic sweaterbox or small glass tank, line the bottom with some wet paper towels, then wad up some more wet paper towels and throw them in too. Add in a waterbowl with a large rock in front of it so the newts can hop in if they wish (also, again, put a small rock *in* the waterbowl, against the edge, so they can crawl out as well), and make sure you wrap the top of the container

PHOTO COURTESY OF HAGEN

There is no harm in giving your newt tank a little visual enhancement by applying some scenic sheeting to the back wall of the tank. These sheets can be purchased at your local pet shop and come in a variety of designs.

with clear plastic wrap so the towels don't dry up too quickly. You will still have to spray-mist this setup every few days, but that's to be expected.

And that's it. Neat, huh? Of course, in the case of the Paludarium Equivalent, you'll be changing the water a heck of a lot more frequently than if you had a filter and all that other stuff, but as I said, the idea here is simplicity; stripping away the frills and getting down to the bare bones. If you have a lot of newts, or a lot of animal tanks in general, then the Generic Equivalent Setups may be just the thing for you. They furnish newts with all they need to live and yet take the strain and responsibility of maintaining a complex tank off your shoulders. Also, they're great for quarantining sick newts; definitely keep that in mind.

PHOTO COURTESY OF AQUARIUM PRODUCTS.

For newt keepers who want to include live plants in their aquatic setup, there is a fertilizing product designed to keep those plants healthy and hardy.

Gravel is probably the best substrate to use with totally aquatic newt species. Shown is the Spanish Ribbed Newt, *Pleurodeles waltl*.

J. PALICKA

FEEDING NEWTS

Perhaps the nicest aspect of newt feeding is the fact that there is a great number of items newts are willing to eat. In fact, it would not be inaccurate to say they are *opportunistic* feeders, which basically means they'll grab anything they can get into their mouths. As long as the item in question is small enough for them to swallow and it doesn't fight back too much, chances are a newt will eat it.

This is, of course, a wonderful characteristic, because it means the keeper will be able to provide his or her newts with a fairly varied diet, and, as many herpetoculturists know, a varied diet is the best kind of diet that can be offered.

FOOD ITEMS

Earthworms

Earthworms are relished by newts and are fairly good for them. It would be untrue to state that earthworms have the potential to be the *only* food item a newt should take, but they are an excellent item nevertheless.

Earthworms can be obtained from a number of places, the most obvious being right from your own backyard. If you have any compost piles, like piles of wet leaves for example, there will

Facing Page: The result of poor keeping—a bloating and orally infected newt, in this case a Hong Kong Warty Newt, *Paramesotriton hongkongensis*. The specimen shown died less than a week after the photograph was taken. Photo: W. P. Mara.

probably be a few billion earthworms at the bottom of it. Along the same lines, you can always dig into some soft, moist earth. During the warmer parts of the year you should be able to garner a few dozen worms with each try (especially after rain).

If you want, you can always set up your own "worm station" by laying down some large pieces of cardboard or wet fabric at the same soft soil locations mentioned before. If you take the time to moisten the cardboard or fabric on a regular basis, you will very probably have worms coming up by the dozen. The darkness and moisture cause mold and so forth to grow, and further causes leaves to decay a little faster, and the molds from this process are what earthworms feed on. After a few weeks you may find your worm supply running low, in which case you will have to move your station elsewhere, continuing this cycle until you reach your initial spot once again, at which time there will very likely be a new supply of worms just waiting to be caught and used as newt food.

If you do not have enough land nearby to utilize this "worm station" idea, you can contact a fisherman's bait and tackle shop and buy worms outright. Remember not to use any manure worms since they are toxic and will hurt your newts; possibly kill them. Also, don't get worms that are incredibly large or else your newts will have trouble dealing with them. You can always chop up large earthworms if you wish, but some folks, find this somewhat gross.

Earthworms can be kept alive in a cool box filled with soft, moist soil and fed on rotting leaf litter, or you can freeze them and thaw them out (by placing them in a bowl of hot water for ten minutes) whenever you need them. If you decide to utilize this latter method, be sure you freeze each earthworm individually. Freezing them together will simply give you one disgusting mass of worm flesh because they will stick to each other.

Small Shrimp

In the fish-keeping hobby there are two types of shrimp that are utilized for food on a standard basis—brine shrimp and ghost shrimp. Brine shrimp are found in inland salt water lakes and are remarkably tiny; newly born specimens are virtually undetectable. Brine shrimp have been cultured for years and are available at almost any pet store that carries fish-keeping supplies. They are very inexpensive, can be bought in quantity, are available virtually all year, and make an excellent meal for newts;

The Spanish Ribbed Newt, *Pleurodeles waltl*, is a fairly reliable eater, going after earthworms, bloodworms, and tiny crickets with admirable fervor.

R. D. BARTLETT

especially smaller newts.

Ghost shrimp are a slightly different story. They earned their name from their ghostly appearance—they are only about an inch long (if that) and are, yes, basically transparent. In fact, I think I'll take a moment out here to say that they are almost as visually fascinating as the newts themselves! Ghost shrimp can also be bought at many pet stores and are, again, very inexpensive and make a fairly good meal. The drawback is that since they are so large, they can only really be offered to fairly large newts. Most newt species seem to enjoy them immensely and I have not experienced any "mishaps" involving ghost shrimp and newts, i.e., a ghost shrimp grabbed a newt and beat it to death then stashed the body behind the filter, etc., but still, some keepers prefer not to take any risks. In my opinion, and based on my experience, ghost shrimp are a fine food item for larger newts.

"Bugs"

I could just use the word "insects" here, but that would leave out a lot of stuff. Spiders, for example, are taken by many newts, but they aren't insects. They are, however, bugs. So are millipedes and centipedes. A plea to entomologists everywhere— please forgive me for my flagrant use of this most offensive word.

This is a broad category, but a good one. Why? Because newts love bugs. As I said in the opening paragraph, newts are opportunistic feeders that will

MICHAEL GILROY

Crickets are accepted by many newt species, but the keeper will usually have to supply either very small crickets, or chop up larger ones.

grab anything they can fit in their mouths. If you have a backyard filled with little bugs, then you have a backyard filled with newt food.

The most common way to get your hands on bugs is by use of a method call "foliage sweeping." In short, the idea is to take a fine mesh net and sweep it through any foliage, transferring anything you catch to a small container. If you find a branch or a leaf infested with bugs, just snip it off and take the whole thing. Inspect what you've caught before giving it to your newts, just in case you've got something that might be harmful to them (like a wasp, for example). Also be sure that the area where you're doing the sweeping has not been treated with any chemicals of any kind.

That, too, will produce a few dead newts.

Finally, always be sure the tank you're throwing these bugs into is very secure. If it isn't, you'll have bugs all over your house.

Strips of Raw Beef

I must admit that I have never given strips of raw beef to any of my own newts, but I have heard of this being done many times in the past.

From the information I've gathered, it seems newts have a real fondness for very small strips of lean beef of the kind that can be bought in any ordinary supermarket. Regardless of the fact that newts will apparently take such an item, I would strongly advise that a keeper not offer it regularly. It should be considered a treat at best, and even then the meat given should be only of the highest quality. The problem with raw beef, and with raw meats of any kind in fact, is that they are simply too fatty for newts to digest. Beef holds very little nutritional value for newts and may cause them many digestive problems. If you must offer it, at least coat the strips with a light sprinkling of multi-vitamin powder. And again, only give beef at distant intervals.

Amphibian Larvae (Tadpoles)

The question here is, who would

Earthworms are relished by virtually all newt species and can be obtained a number of ways. Notice the worm in the lower left corner of this photo of a tankful of Spanish Ribbed Newts, *Pleurodeles waltl.*

R. D. BARTLETT

MICHAEL GILROY

Bloodworms are available at most any pet store and are taken with great eagerness by most newts, especially aquatic types. Bloodworms can be bought live or frozen, but newts seem to prefer the former.

want to use amphibian larvae for food? The fact, however, is that most newts love amphibian larvae, i.e., small frog tadpoles, which can be acquired with some regularity through the right channels (some pet stores, private breeders, biological supply houses, etc.). Furthermore, tadpoles are very nutritious. They can, however, tend to be a little expensive. Contact a local herpetocultural society and see who you can get in touch with.

Bloodworms, Whiteworms, *Tubifex*, Etc.

Again, anyone involved in the fish-keeping field will recognize any of these items. They are the tiny worms used in so many facets of fish-feeding.

Bloodworms look like fat, tiny squiggles and can be purchased at almost any pet store, very inexpensively. They are usually sold by weight and are an excellent food for newts.

Whiteworms can also be purchased inexpensively and in quantity from most pet stores, but they are not as good for newts as bloodworms are. They tend to be a little higher in fat and are a little more lacking in calcium. They are a supplementary item at best, but

MICHAEL GILROY

Larval newts can also be fed bloodworms, and feeding them via a "worm cup" (as shown here) is a very sensible approach and is highly recommended.

hardly a staple food.

Finally, *Tubifex* worms, which many people recognize by their similar brand name, are very tiny, about three-quarters of an inch in length, and appear as tiny red squiggles. They live in the muddy bottoms of ditches and streams, where they are buried mostly in the mud, but with enough of their bodies sticking out to gain oxygen from the water. They can be purchased at pet stores in large quantities and are always very inexpensive. They can also be bought frozen, and, in many ways, frozen *Tubifex* are superior

to live because you won't have to care for them. Many newts, however, will not accept frozen and thawed *Tubifex*, but if yours do, you're in luck. If not, keep the live ones in a container of cool shallow water.

One final note on *Tubifex*—if you are ambitious enough, you can actually collect them from the wild by first finding a muddy-bottomed water body, then grabbing clumps of the mud and bringing it home with you. By placing the mud in a steel container and hovering it over a low flame, you will drive the worms to the surface. Or, place the mud outside overnight so it has the chance to dry up. Then, the next morning, split the dried mud open and the worms should be in a ball inside.

Guppies/Small Fish

One item that most any keeper can get a hold of is a guppy or other small fish. Newts generally accept guppies and small fish and such meals are really quite good for them. Again, either of these items can be purchased at any pet store, in quantity, and for a very low price. Keep in mind, of course, that the fish you buy shouldn't be too large, not only because the newts won't be able to eat them, but because they might eat the newts!

Also, if your newts are willing to accept this, it is possible to freeze a large fish and portion out into small pieces when needed. If you are lucky enough to have newts that will go for it, remember that saltwater fish varieties should not be used. The salt is just too alien to the newts's systems and will cause them great harm.

Water Fleas/*Daphnia*

Again, this item can be obtained at many pet stores and is very inexpensive. It is worth noting that *Daphnia* is not the only genus referred to as a "water flea," but it is probably the name most often used when asking for water fleas for purchase. Water fleas are remarkably tiny (up to about a quarter of an inch) and are usually taken very eagerly by newts. They are indeed a good addition to their diet and are highly recommended.

Vitamin Supplements

As with any other captive herptile, newts will benefit greatly from the occasional vitamin supplement.

Today, since herpetoculture is so popular, there are a great many vitamin supplement products on the market specially designed to aid the keeper. The most reasonable of these is the vitamin powder. What a keeper should do is sprinkle the powder onto whatever food item he or she is going to give to the newts, and then offer the item when the newts are particularly hungry. I point this out because if you cover an earthworm with vitamin powder and your newts aren't all that hungry, you'll drop the item in the tank and the powder will either dissolve in the water or the item will rot on the land.

HOW MUCH FOOD AND HOW OFTEN?

Newts are fairly hardy creatures and thus don't have to be fed everyday. In fact, I don't feel they even need to be fed every other day. What I have always done, and with results that I have always been satisfied with (my newts are still alive to this day, so I must be doing something correctly), is give each newt a good-sized meal every five days. By good-sized I mean about twice as much as I think they can accept at one time. For example, I have one 10-gallon tank that has three adult newts in it. Every five days, I dump in a cupful of live *Tubifex*, a cupful being about a half of a full measuring cup's worth (not that you'd use one of your kitchen measuring cups for such a lovely purpose). The worms, naturally, integrate themselves into the gravel bedding, and the newts simply draw from them whenever they feel like it. It is part of an ideology I strongly believe in concerning herp husbandry—let the animal(s) have as much freedom of decision as possible concerning all parts of their existence. Don't give them whatever amounts of food *you* think they'll want to eat; give them a good supply and let them decide. Newts aren't like many other herptiles in the sense that they will eat themselves into obesity. They seem to have a natural sense of what's "enough." At least that has always been my observation.

Daphnia make a good meal for most newts, particularly small newts. *Daphnia* can be obtained at any of the better pet shops (usually frozen), or you can collect them yourself on the surfaces of ponds.

D. UNTERGASSER

BREEDING NEWTS

The breeding of newts in captivity is really not all that difficult of an affair, but it does require some serious attention to detail and therefore is perhaps best left to either the professional herpetoculturist or the highly ambitious amateur. I will attempt to give the reader as much basic information as possible, so, at the very least, he or she will be able to details that are to be found therein may very well make or break any of your attempts.

THE COOLING PERIOD

Almost all newts must go through a period of reduced temperature before they can be induced to breed. Since newts are fairly cold-environment creatures to begin with (in comparison to

R. D. BARTLETT

The breeding of newts is not a difficult affair. Some species, like these Spanish Ribbed Newts, *Pleurodeles waltl*, have been bred in captivity for many years.

make some competent attempts, but in order to improve your grip on the subject, it is strongly suggested that you expose yourself to as much natural reproductive history information as possible concerning whichever particular newt species you happen to have. Some of the finer other herptiles), this period of rest sometimes requires alarmingly low temperatures.

In captivity, this can be most easily provided during the winter months. If you do not live in an area where the winters get all that cold, you can try putting your newts in a refrigerator. The ideal

W. P. MARA

Sexual dimorphism is sometimes determinable by the shape of the tail. In these California Newts, *Taricha torosa*, for example, the male, on the left, has the broader tail.

not want to be disturbed.

Be sure to monitor the hibernating newts's ambient temperature, and if it goes too low, provide some sort of heat source. Needless to say, a newt left in too low a temperature will become a "newtsickle." Don't let this happen. If you feel you won't be able to check the temperature everyday, set up your heat source, whether it be a fully submersible heater with the aquatic species or a simple ceramic room heater for the terrestrial species, in conjunction with a reliable thermostat.

The average period of hibernation for newts should be about six to eight weeks. This can vary from species to species (again, research the natural history), but not too much.

SETTING UP THE BREEDING TANK

temperature for the newts discussed in this book is around 46°F/8°C, give or take a few degrees.

Hibernation chambers should be set up with attention to simplicity. For terrestrial species, a plastic sweaterbox filled with about three inches of soil and a few flat rocks will do fine. For aquatic species, the same sweaterbox except filled with water and a thick gravel substrate is adequate. Both chambers should be darkened during the hibernation period; the newts will

All the newts discussed in this book breed in the water and breed during the spring. Since the newts you will be keeping will not be attuned to the presence of spring in the wild, for your purposes, spring is defined as whenever you take them out of hibernation. You could have spring in the fall if you felt like it! Keep in mind, however, that many older, wild-caught specimens will have developed fairly acute biorhythms and may not be easily fooled. Therefore, do yourself a favor and begin your captive breeding season during the time that is closest to that of the newts's season in the wild.

Once you take the newts out of hibernation, you need to set up their breeding tank. This is not difficult, and is very close to the paludarium setup discussed in the housing chapter—it will be mostly water, but with only one or two rocks that reach above the surface to act as land bodies, and with live plants as a necessity (some keepers claim they can use artificial plants, but it's not worth taking the chance, especially since real aquatic plants are so inexpensive to begin with).

The water temperature should be somewhere in the neighborhood of about 68°F/ 20°C, but the real idea is that the entire environment around the newts becomes noticeably warmer to them, and furthermore, the photoperiod becomes longer. These are the two triggers that will get them going. You can of course provide warm water and extended light very easily through the use of fully submersible heaters (if necessary) and fluorescent lights attached to timers.

THE BREEDING PROCESS

If you really want to get some good breeding results from your newts, make sure the males outnumber the females by about

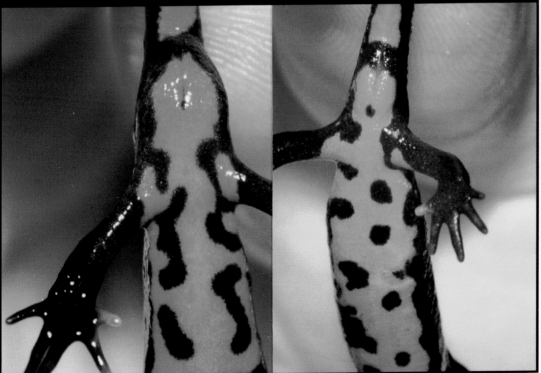

During the breeding season, a keeper can usually tell the males from the females by the shape of the cloacas—those of the adult males (left) should be swollen.

W. P. MARA

W. P. MARA

Gravid female newts can be distinguished fairly easily during the later stages of their gestation—their bellies will be greatly swollen. Specimen shown is a California Newt, *Taricha torosa.*

the hopes of breeding them one day, you can cover yourself and improve your chances by acquiring as many as is practically possible for you.Otherwise, it really is just a matter of good fortune.

The process is simple—place all your adult "breeder" newts into the breeding tank, and just wait. Sometimes events won't transpire immediately, so if you wish to observe you may have to be very patient. There are a number of different procedures involved, depending on which species you're dealing with, but for the most part they are fairly similar. The male will try to arouse the female, then he will grab the female or be grasped from above, and, eventually, he will release his spermatophore, which will be picked up by the female with her cloaca.

Once the pair are finished breeding, remove the males and place them back in their original home. If you have placed more than one female into the breeding tank, you may want to separate them and set them up in their own individual tanks. Why? Because once any eggs are laid, there is a chance one of the females might eat them. It's difficult enough making sure you're around to separate a single mother from her eggs, but when you've got a whole tank full of females to keep an eye on, the problem increases. If you decide to take my advice and set up a few individual tanks, remember to set them up in the same fashion as the breeding tank—with live

three to one. You can tell the sexes apart because the males, during the breeding season, will be very swollen around the cloacal region. Furthermore, depending on the species you have, many males will develop dark nuptial pads on their hands and feet, plus some of them will develop very conspicuous dorsal crests. It should be pointed out that males and females really can't be delineated when they are young; only sexually mature adults can be separated. If you are going to purchase some young newts in plants in particular because many of the females will need these in order to lay their eggs on. A 10-gallon tank is ideal for this type of setup. As soon as the eggs are laid, remove the female and place her back into her "normal" tank. This, of course, must be done fairly carefully, so it is advised that you make use of an aquarist's fish-catching net. Also, remember that some species of females will lay a number of egg cltches over a period of months, so you may want to shift the eggs into separate tanks rather than the females. If you wish to do this, again, use a fishnet for any loose eggs, or, in the case of eggs that have adhere to aquatic plants, move the plants themselves. The tank setup, naturally should be identical to the tank from which they were removed.

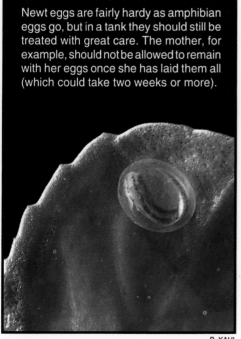

Newt eggs are fairly hardy as amphibian eggs go, but in a tank they should still be treated with great care. The mother, for example, should not be allowed to remain with her eggs once she has laid them all (which could take two weeks or more).

B. KAHL

CARING FOR THE EGGS

Caring for the eggs is not a problem for the keeper. There's really not much more to do beyond keeping an eye on the water's temperature to make sure it doesn't fluctuate too much. Furthermore, be sure that the filter your using isn't too "rough." What I mean by this is, some filters seem fairly violent with the water they are in and will create a great amount of current. Newt eggs are fairly hardy, but the less disturbance the better. There are a great many filters on the pet market today that are so gentle they hardly make any noise at all and almost seem like they're not even running. These are the kind I would recommend for use with newt egg tanks.

CARING FOR THE LARVAE

Once the eggs hatch, the larvae will have to be fed on some very small foods indeed. *Daphnia*, *Cyclops*, chopped bloodworms, chopped whiteworms, chopped *Tubifex*, etc., are all acceptable. In truth, newt larvae are actually rather hardy and seem very willing to take meals; it is just a matter of being able to provide them with what they need. The key to remember is that their diet is really not all that different from the adults's, but it has to be offered in a form in which it can be swallowed. Some keepers have suggested using certain fish foods, but I choose to stick with what I feel is more natural to them. Experiment with different things until you come across what works best for both you and the "newtlings;" that is the ultimate suggestion.

METAMORPHOSIS

When metamorphosis time draws near, it is very, very important that you provide the larvae with some land areas onto which they can climb when they transform. If you do not do this, most of the newly transformed newts will die (in time, almost all of them will, but a very select few, depending on the species, will remain larvae and may never transform). Of course, in the case of those species which remain aquatic throughout their lives, the provision of a land body is totally unnecessary, but with the others, it is a must. The land body only needs to break the waters surface and, again, as I mentioned before, it should be easy to get to.

CARING FOR NEWLY TRANSFORMED YOUNG

Once the larvae have transformed, they can begin their lives as normal newts. Those species that are terrestrial should be placed in a terrarium setup of their own (not with adults) and fed a normal newt diet which should, again, be offered in very small portions so they won't have any trouble getting it into their mouths. Aquatic newts can also be sustained on a normal adult diet given in smaller portions. Most species mature in about two to three years.

Photo of a recently hatched Northern Crested Newt, *Triturus cristatus*, larvae. Such larvae must be fed on very small items, such as chopped bloodworms, *Tubifex*, *Daphnia*, and so on.

MICHAEL GILROY

THE FIRE SALAMANDER, *SALAMANDRA SALAMANDRA*

I thought it would be a good idea to include a quick chapter on the Fire Salamander, *Salamandra salamandra*, for two reasons—one, it is, like all the other animals discussed in this book, a member of the family Salamandridae, and two, it seems to be enormously popular in the amphibian-keeping hobby. I'll try to cover as many topics about it as I can, and hopefully, from what I've written, you'll be able to successfully maintain one without any problems whatsoever. It has never held the reputation for being a particularly difficult terrarium subject to begin with, so in many ways an interested hobbyist already has an advantage.

NATURAL HISTORY

First described by Linnaeus way back in 1758 (under a different name at the time), the Fire Salamander occurs in northwestern Africa, and central and southern Europe to western Asia, making it a fairly widespread creature in the Palearctic Region. It is a creatures of damp woodland areas and spends its days hiding among moss beds, rocks, leaf litter, under decaying logs, in tree stumps, or in burrows. It grows to almost 12 in/ 30 cm and its base color is usually black with yellow marbling, although on many specimens there is much more yellow (or goldish yellow) than black. The beautiful coloration not only makes it a visually compelling animal, but warns would-be predators to keep away (or else the Fire Salamander, once grasped in an animal's mouth, will release a sticky fluid that is definitely very distasteful to almost all creatures). There are two longitudinal stripes on the dorsum, and the tail is round. A parotid gland can be seen on either side of the head and there are further rows of glands along the dorsum and laterum. There are a great many subspecies in the group—over two dozen—but the validity of many of these has been questioned through the years.

The reproductive cycle of the Fire Salamander is most interesting. It takes place entirely on land, but is, in many ways, similar to that of the Ribbed Newts, genus *Pleurodeles*. The male grasps the female from behind, then drops his spermatophore, further stimulating her into picking it up by rubbing her cloaca and throat. Mating takes place either in the summer or the fall, depending on the elevation of the population. Once the female has taken in the spermatophore, she will deposit anywhere from 40 to 70 larvae into slow-moving streams or other nearby water sources, and these larvae are already greatly developed. In some cases, although rarely, this species has

M. P. AND C. PIEDNOIR

The Fire Salamander, *Salamandra salamandra*, has been catching hobbyists's eyes for years. In its genus there is only one other species, *Salamandra atra*, which gives birth to fully transformed young.

been known to give birth to fully developed young, already in their terrestrial stage and ready to live life to the fullest.

HOUSING

Perhaps the central reason the Fire Salamander is so popular is because it is so amazingly hardy; you'd really have to go out of your way to kill one off in captivity. It's housing requirements, for example, are minimal.

They need to be set up in a terrarium; refer to the housing chapter for the basic approach. Beyond that, you should include a thick sheaf of sphagnum moss as a hiding place rather than a bunch of rocks. Also, mist the tank every few days, but don't use plastic wrap over the top of the

tank to hold in moisture. They do indeed need moisture, but to try and replicate a rainforest atmosphere is unnecessary. Climate control is also quite simple—room temperature is fine.

FEEDING

Again, the keeper is in luck with the Fire Salamander, because the feeding aspect of its husbandry is just as easy as its housing. In a word, Fire Salamanders seem to eat *anything*. You can refer to the feeding chapter of this book for most of the items, but there are one or two more that weren't even included. Pinkie mice, for example, are not only easy to acquire, but they provide a Fire Salamander with a good meal as well. Remember, however, that pinkie mice should only be offered to only the larger specimens; smaller Fire Salamanders won't even be able to get them into their mouths. Beyond that, crickets, spiders, earthworms, and whole variety of other insects will be gladly accepted, but beware that although most Fire Salamanders are hardy eaters, some are very shy and will only feed during the night hours. That, then, obviously is the best time to offer the food.

BREEDING

Fire Salamanders have been bred quite a number of times in captivity, even in the United States where captive salamander and newt breeding is about as lively as a cemetery on a cold winter's night.

The captive mating itself is really most interesting. The male will slip himself under the female and, if he has to, carry her around on his back for quite some time, rubbing the female's cloaca in order to stimulate her. When she is ready, which she will signal by doing a mild sort of wiggle, the male rubs her throat with his head and simultaneously releases the spermatophore, then moves his posterior to one side so the female can pick it up.

She will hold this packet and the eggs inside for the remainder of the season. The following spring, the keeper will have to provide a large water body for the female because she will then be ready to lay her larvae in it. The larvae will already have tails, legs, and all that other good stuff, and measure about 1.2 in/30 mm long. The female should not, after giving birth, be allowed near the young for she may decide to make a meal out of them. Furthermore, it is best that you keep the young as separate from each other for basically the same reason. You also don't want to competition for food to get too heady or else you will have some very healthy larvae, and beyond that, a few dead ones. Feed them on cyclops, daphnia, *Tubifex*, whiteworms (chopped), bloodworms, etc. These larvae are, like their parents, quite hardy and willing to eat. Depending on what you set the water temperature at, the larvae should begin to transform in between three and five months. When this starts to take place, the tail fin and the external gills will begin to regress. It is during this time that you must provide land areas for them to climb upon— large rocks that just break the water's surface will do fine (as long, of course, as the rocks are of a gently sloping nature. Don't make the climb too hard for them!) Newly transformed Fire Salamanders are about 2 in/5 cm long and can live in a terrarium setup that is normal for the species. Feed them on tiny insects, chopped earthworms, small spiders, and so on. They will reach sexual maturity in about three and a half years.

SUGGESTED READING

H-1102, 830 pages, Over 1800 color photos

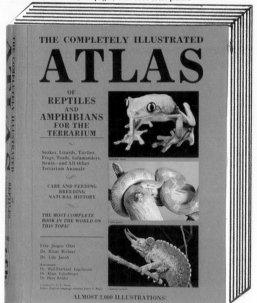

TS-182, 192 pgs. 175 color photos

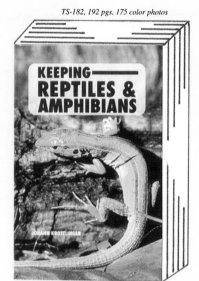

KD-006
(hard cover),
KD-006S
(soft cover)
64 pages
230 color
photos

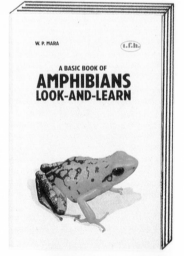

PS-876, 384 pages,
175 color photos

H-935, 576 pages,
260 color photos

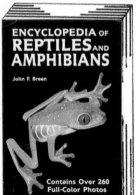

TW-116, 256 pages,
167 color photos

INTRODUCING GROUND BOAS

A MIXED GROUP

For at least a decade the boas have been the prize of snake keeping. Everything from the common Boa Constrictor to the rarest Madagascan boas and Caribbean slender boas finds a ready market among both beginners and advanced hobbyists. Often the trend is to think that "bigger is better," and hobbyists may compete for the biggest Boa Constrictor or Green Anaconda,

Candoia, the island boas or Solomons ground-boas of the subfamily Boinae. Because hobbyists look at form more than anatomy, we'll also talk a little bit about three other small burrowers that have been treated variously as boas, pythons, and even members of unique families, the "pseudo-boa" genera *Loxocemus*, *Calabaria*, and *Xenopeltis*. I am well aware that we're getting pretty broad in

C. BANKS

Many small boas, such as the attractive Rough-scaled Sand-Boa, *Eryx conicus*, are available and are keepable by even the beginning hobbyist with little money and room.

regardless of the complications involved in keeping big, often dangerous snakes. But the hobbyist with a desire for a nice boa doesn't have to settle for a big snake to enjoy the thrill of keeping a boa, not when some beautiful and easy to keep ground boas are available on the market.

The ground boas for the purposes of this book are a miscellaneous group of rather small boas from around the world. Here we'll include not only the members of the boid subfamily Erycinae (the Rosy Boa, Rubber Boa, and sand-boas) but

choosing snakes to cover in a little book, but I believe that to hobbyists they form a rather tight group of similar-looking burrowing snakes that have similar problems and joys.

CONTENTS

This book will cover the following genera of ground boas and "pseudo-boas." Most of the genera are monotypic (they contain only a single species), but a few have several species. Common names are my selection because many of these groups have a great number of names in the hobby literature.

G. P. MERKER

Rosy Boas, *Lichanura trivirgata*, are among the most beautiful of the pet snakes and are very easy to keep if you remember to keep them dry.

•*Calabaria*, burrowing pythons. One species.

•*Candoia*, ground-boas. Three species.

•*Charina*, rubber boas. One species.

•*Eryx*, sand-boas. About ten species.

•*Lichanura*, rosy boas. One species.

•*Loxocemus*, neotropical pythons. One species.

•*Xenopeltis*, sunbeam snakes. Two species.

Actually, the way the taxonomy of the boas and pythons is changing at the moment, it is conceivable that all these small, usually burrowing primitive snakes might just end up related after all. (Island boas are an exception, being close relatives of the American tree-boas and boa constrictor.) Until several herpetologists started looking closely at the relationships of the boas and pythons and the several similar groups of snakes, the usual system was to have one large family Boidae with two subfamilies (Boinae and Pythoninae) plus a separate family or subfamily for *Loxocemus* (Loxocemidae or Loxoceminae of Boidae) and a separate family for *Xenopeltis* (Xenopeltidae). *Calabaria* was considered to be a close relative of the Ball Python slightly modified for burrowing. The other genera were placed in the Boinae (true boas) but in separate tribes, *Candoia* in Boini and the others in Erycini.

Now no one is sure exactly where any of the pythons and boas and their allies fit into a classification scheme. Several different—and I mean drastically different—classifications now are being proposed by reputable herpetologists for the pythons and boas, including various mixes of families and subfamilies that would be unfamiliar to any hobbyist and most professional herpetologists. I'm not going to waste your time going over these classifications because I can't tell yet which will "take" and which will be forgotten next week.

TERRARIUM REQUIREMENTS

The boas we are discussing in this book will fall naturally into two different lifestyles: most are burrowers, but the Solomons ground-boas seldom are found underground and sometimes even climb trees and shrubs. Most are inhabitants of often cool and relatively dry savannahs or true deserts, but *Candoia* and *Calabaria* like it more humid. Because few of these snakes exceed 3 feet or so in length (though some *Candoia* females may reach 6 feet in a few instances), they usually can be accommodated in a simple all-glass terrarium or similar cage. A 20-gallon tank will give most specimens plenty of room to cruise around in during their

Organic substrates are ideal for snakes. Most are easy to work with, pleasing to the eye, and obtainable in bulk quantities. Photo courtesy of Coralife/Energy Savers.

evening and early morning activity periods. Substrates can be kept as simple as you like. Many hobbyists like to use newspaper as the substrate because it can be replaced easily and cheaply, but a more natural base would be 3 to 6 inches of loose dry mulch or orchid bark, often with sphagnum moss added. Sand-boas (*Eryx*) like a thick layer of plain coarse sand, while *Candoia* like sphagnum. Keep the terrarium dry unless you are keeping *Candoia* or *Calabaria*.

Although almost all these snakes will become active during the day if they like their surroundings, they need little in the way of special lighting or even basking areas. Pregnant females will bask more than males, and it never hurts to provide a warm basking rock; "dark light" heat emitters work well. A heating pad under the cage will provide all the heat you need for most species, though sand-boas, the Rosy Boa, *Calabaria*, and *Candoia* like it a bit warmer than room temperature.

All terraria for burrowing boas should be provided with hideboxes, rocks, slabs of bark, overturned flowerpots, and similar retreats. Though not especially shy, these boas like to hide and burrow most of the day and as a general rule will not adapt unless you make them as comfortable as possible.

FEEDING

With some exceptions, the ground boas can be trained to take frozen and thawed mice of appropriate sizes. The exceptions are mostly young specimens that prefer cold-blooded prey, especially lizards and frogs. Not uncommonly, even adults may go on hunger strikes and only come out if offered lizards and frogs. A few adults of any species, especially those that are wild-caught, may never adapt to frozen rodents.

BREEDING

All the ground boas give livebirth, but our three "pseudo-boa" add-ons all lay eggs (which is one of the among the most difficult to breed of the pythons and boas, with few or no successful hatchings in captivity being recorded.

Except for the sunbeam snakes and females of a few other species, the ground boas and "pseudo-boas" have spurs on each side of the vent. Males usually have larger spurs than females and also have the typical "hemipenis bulge" of most male snakes. Mating may occur underground in extreme burrowers

PHOTO COURTESY OF CORALIFE/ENERGY SAVERS

There are a number of specialty products available in pet shops that allow you to gain a better grasp on the more subtle aspects of snake keeping.

reasons why they often have been considered to be pythons or python relatives). Some of these snakes are bred regularly by commercial breeders and amateurs alike (especially *Lichanura* and some of the *Eryx* species), but others are of virtually unknown breeding habits. All three of our "pseudo-boas" are or on the surface of the ground. The male uses his spurs to make the female raise her tail so mating can occur. Young are born some four to six months later and usually take their first meal after their first molt.

OK, so much for generalities. Now on with the boa show!

RUBBER BOAS

When we think of boas we often think of animals of the tropics or at least of the warm subtropics. This actually is not true today and has not been true for several million years. Fossil boas of various types, some possibly related to genera living today, are found over much of the United States and southern Canada, and at one time there must have been a thriving fauna of large and small boas in Nebraska and Florida, living among giant tortoises, monitor-like lizards, giant alligator lizards, strange salamanders, and equally strange water turtles. Though these all became extinct in the eastern United States over a million years ago, one cold-adapted boa still exists in the western United States and southwestern Canada, the Rubber Boa, *Charina bottae*.

This species is little changed from what seems to be its fossil ancestor, *Charina prebottae* of the Miocene (probably some 5 to 10 million years ago), and occupies much the same range. The Rubber Boa is found in coniferous forests of most of the Northwest, including southern British Columbia, south into central California and Utah, with apparently isolated populations from Montana into central Wyoming. Additional isolated populations are found at higher elevations in southern California. No subspecies currently are recognized, though two additional names were familiar in the literature just a decade ago. This is the most northerly boa unless one of the Asian sand-boas, close relatives incidentally, reaches as far north into Siberia.

As might be expected from the northern range, this is a snake that tolerates humid, cold weather and even may be active in light snow and at just a few degrees above freezing. In much of its range even the summers are cool and wet, yet in other parts of its territory it occurs in the dry, hot rolling grasslands in the foothills near the Pacific Ocean. It is an amazingly adaptable animal that burrows and climbs and even swims well.

The Rubber Boa is a very small boa, usually 20 to 26 inches long and with a rare maximum length of about 33 inches. Females usually are a few inches longer than males in the same population. The common name comes from the "rubbery" appearance of living specimens that is hard to explain in words but becomes obvious when you see a specimen. The snakes also are amazingly

K. H. SWITAK

Heads or tails? Rubber Boas, *Charina bottae*, are especially notorious for having tails that look and act like heads.

flexible, the rounded head and tail able to move in all directions. When disturbed, a newly captured specimen may form a tight ball with the head in the center and the tail on the outside and acting like a head. The short, very rounded tail ends in a large plate and is prehensile, aiding in climbing. The rounded head is covered with relatively regular plates that often fragment but are never as irregular as in the Rubber Boa.

Adult Rubber Boas generally are some shade of olive brown, often quite greenish, to pale tan, the belly paler and sometimes mottled with orangish or grayish. Newborns start off pinkish to bright pinkish tan and gradually darken as they grow. The whole snake appears quite bright and somewhat iridescent and is quite attractive in a subdued way.

TERRARIUM CARE

Keeping Rubber Boas, especially captive-breds and half-grown wild-caught specimens, is not difficult. They do well at room temperature during most of the year, with an undertank heating pad and a basking rock for good measure though neither will be used much. The substrate should be at least 4 to 6 inches of good grade mulch or orchid bark, anything that the snake can freely burrow through. Provide hiding places and a water bowl. Most Rubber Boas grow up in a moist environment, so spray the terrarium liberally twice a week to keep the substrate moist but never wet. Preferably the snake should have the opportunity to choose wetter and drier parts of the terrarium. As usual with the ground boas, special

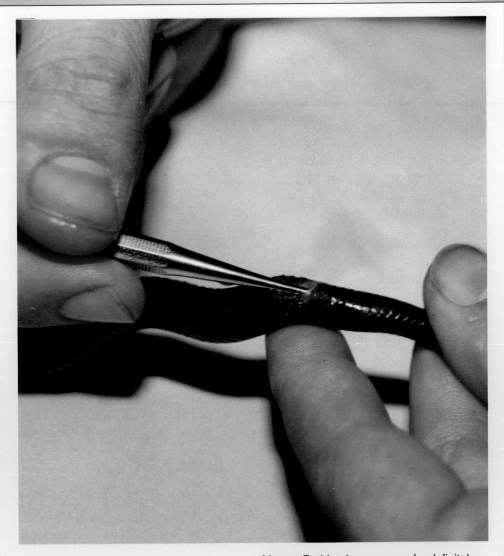

Facing page: Though not especially colorful snakes, Rubber Boas, *Charina bottae*, are gentle boas that can be easy to keep if you get a specimen that feeds well. Photo by R. D. Bartlett.

Above: Probing is necessary for definitely determining the sex of most snakes. In boas the probe usually extends about 10 to 12 scale rows into the hemipenis pouch, while in females the cloacal glands only allow the probe to go about three rows down. Probing can be dangerous and must be learned at the hands of an experienced keeper. Photo by W. P. Mara.

Though the exact number and placement of the head scales may vary quite a bit, in the Rubber Boa, *Charina bottae*, there always are large, relatively regular plates on the head. Photo by K. Lucas.

lighting is not required unless you try to keep plants in the terrarium.

Though some Rubber Boas refuse to feed in captivity, especially very young and adult specimens, many adapt quickly to a diet of pinkies and fuzzies. Remember that the mouth of these little boas is quite small and not very flexible, so try to match the size of the food with the size of the snake. Prey are killed by constriction or crushing against the burrow wall. It may be necessary to feed living

pockets so at best only the pointed tips project. Like many "normal" snakes such as kingsnakes and rat snakes, Rubber Boas must be overwintered to be successfully bred. They can be kept from late December or January until March at a temperature of 50 to 55°F (10 to 13°C) and then slowly returned to normal temperatures (about 75°F, 24°C). Of course their gut must be emptied before overwintering starts and it helps to have a water bowl in

PHOTO COURTESY OF OCEAN NUTRITION

Many keepers prefer to give their snakes frozen-and-thawed mice rather than live (for safety reasons, i.e., a dead mouse can't injure a snake). Such mice are now available in packages at your local pet shop.

mice at first before the boa switches over to frozen and thawed food. Additionally, in nature these snakes feed on frogs, lizards, salamanders, and probably large invertebrates; it's quite an omnivore, which might be used to advantage to get difficult specimens to feed in captivity.

Breeding has succeeded often in captivity, and second-generation specimens have been produced. Males are easily distinguished by their relatively large and obvious spurs on either side of the vent, while the spurs of the female are small and mostly hidden in scale

the terrarium so the snakes can drink if they awaken a bit. Mating occurs in nature and in the terrarium from April through May, resulting in litters of three to eight young delivered in August and September. The young are about 7 inches in length, and their bright color makes them a fascinating sight.

In nature females breed about every third year, but in the confines of the terrarium breeding may occur every year. Maturity takes three or four years for males, a year longer for females. Specimens over 20 inches should be sexually mature, except

H. KENDITZ

Rubber Boas, *Charina bottae*, have loose skin and a peculiar rubbery feel that has given them their common name. Don't be misled though—these are quite powerful snakes like all the ground boas, and they also climb well. A secure terrarium cover is a must.

perhaps specimens from the mountains of southern California, which seem to seldom exceed 16 inches in adult length. These are long-lived snakes, as you might expect from their slow maturity, usually living 10 to 12 years in the terrarium, with wild females 20 years old known to have produced young.

At one time Rubber Boas used to be regularly available in the pet shops, though they seldom survived well. Usually the specimens offered were full adults that failed to adapt to the rather primitive terrarium conditions offered just 10 or 20 years ago. Babies have always been hard to feed in captivity and even today babies born in captivity may refuse to feed and have to be overwintered without having fed. This seems to be rather normal behavior, in fact, for the species as the babies usually survive well and come out of hibernation with an appetite for frogs and pinkies. Though not a colorful species, the Rubber Boa is truly unique in appearance and

fascinating because of its adaptation to extreme conditions. As the most northern boa it is unique and an American treasure.

Unfortunately, Rubber Boas are no longer that easy to obtain. Captive-breds are not readily available on the market and wild-caughts have a poor reputation as being delicate and non-feeders, so they are not heavily marketed (perhaps for the best). In most of its range this is a snake of what is popularly known as "old growth forests," where it is found along with Spotted Owls and other environmentalist rallying points. Whether Rubber Boa populations are

Newborn Rubber Boas, *Charina bottae*, are much brighter in color than the parents, often tending toward bright pink with yellow bellies. They soon begin to darken into the more olive brown to chocolate brown adults, however. Unfortunately, many young Rubber Boas do not feed well at first and may have to be put into hibernation (now more formally known as brumation as it applies to reptiles and amphibians) without having fed. Most begin to feed when temperatures climb the next spring. Photo by K. H. Switak.

decreasing as a result of logging and other human activities in the Northwest is uncertain, but this boa has a tradition of living well near humans.

If you should run across a Rubber Boa at the local pet shop (it happens!) and you have a spare terrarium, this boa certainly can justify using the room. If you are aware of the possible feeding problem of wild-caught adults and very young specimens you should be able to find some way to get around it. If you can buy a captive-bred yearling, you should have it easy. Give this little boa a try and you might be pleasantly surprised.

Above: If you can find either a captive-bred Rubber Boa or a legally wild-caught half-grown specimen that eats, you could have a very nice and long-lived pet boa that needs minimal care and space. Photo by M. Panzella.

Facing Page: Young Rubber Boas, *Charina bottae*, often are much brighter than the adults. The two young shown here are toward the bright dark brown end of the color spectrum, especially as compared to the olive mother in the bottom photo. Top photo by P. Freed. Bottom photo by K. H. Switak.

Mexican Rosy Boas, *Lichanura trivirgata trivirgata*, have a distinctive pattern of nearly black stripes on a cream or pale khaki background. Photo by K. H. Switak.

Facing Page: Much less cleanly marked is the subspecies of Rosy Boa from southern California, now known as *Lichanura trivirgata myriolepis*. These can be very variable snakes. Photo by F. J. Dodd.

ROSY BOAS

The southwestern corner of the United States plus Baja California and western Sonora, Mexico, is the home of one of the most popular boas in the terrarium hobby today, *Lichanura trivirgata*, the Rosy Boa. This distinctively striped little (usually 2 to 3 feet in total length, always less than 4 feet long) burrowing boa is closely related to the Rubber Boa but distinctively different in structure as well as coloration. In addition to stripes versus uniform olive coloration, the top of the head in *Lichanura* is covered with numerous small, irregular scales, never a few large plates as in *Charina*. The snout of the Rosy Boa is longer and more "normal" in shape, while the tail, though still relatively blunt, is moderately pointed. A stout-bodied species, the Rosy Boa is a powerful constrictor like all the other ground boas and feeds mostly on small mammals in nature.

For years there have been enthusiasts who liked to keep Rosy Boas and even breed them on occasion, but only in the last decade or so have numbers hit the market and commercially bred specimens become common, though still expensive. Even more recently hobbyists have begun to specialize in the various geographically restricted color patterns typical of this species, trying to keep breeding lines pure and uniform. In fact, quite a controversy has arisen over what are the proper subspecific names for the various patterns in the species.

Because taxonomy is important in the Rosy Boa and affects both how the hobbyist pairs the snakes for breeding and their price and

desirability, I'll have to spend some time on the subspecies problem in this snake, but first we'll cover keeping and breeding.

KEEPING

Simply put, keeping a Rosy Boa is a cinch if you follow a few basic rules. Remember that in nature these are snakes of dry, warm savannahs and hills, often found under rocks and logs. They are not really desert-dwellers, but they do well in a terrarium with a substrate of sand. Many keepers prefer to use other substrate materials such as corncob granules and wood chips (not cedar) for the substrate. Anything will work as long as it is deep enough (2 to 4 inches or so) for the snake to burrow into when it wants to disappear.

Although a 20-gallon terrarium will work well as a cage, there is a problem because the Rosy Boa does not like high humidities. In many parts of the United States and in Europe, the normal summer relative humidity may reach 90% or more for weeks at a time, leading to a decline in the general health of a Rosy Boa forced to live through a warm, humid spell. If you live in such an area you should consider a more open terrarium with one or two walls as well as the lid composed mostly of mesh that allows adequate

This striking colored Rosy Boa appears to be intermediate between *Lichanura trivirgata trivirgata* and *L. t. saslowi* in color. Boas from Baja California often are imported but many more are bred in captivity.

R. D. BARTLETT

R. D. BARTLETT

Rosy Boas such as this *Lichanura trivirgata myriolepis* from southern California are adapted to warm, dry conditions. High humidity may be your worst enemy when keeping these snakes.

ventilation and thus a reduced humidity in the cage. For the same reason a water bowl is not recommended for the Rosy Boa cage. Any spills could increase the humidity beyond acceptable limits (perhaps 60% RH). Either provide a drinking bowl one day per week and then remove it or let the snake have water only while you are there to watch it drink contentedly and then remove the bowl.

Rosys like it fairly warm, certainly 80°F (27°C) or more, most of the year. Undertank heating works well, as does a basking light over a flat rock. Much of the snake's day is spent under the substrate, and it will use a hot rock heater that is covered with flat rocks or a hidebox. Provide plenty of cover such as cork bark pieces and low hideboxes. Many Rosy Boas like to climb, so a branch or two will not go to waste. Terrarium lighting is not that important, so use the normal combination of fluorescent lights in a reflector, which will help air movement in the terrarium a bit as well.

R. D. BARTLETT

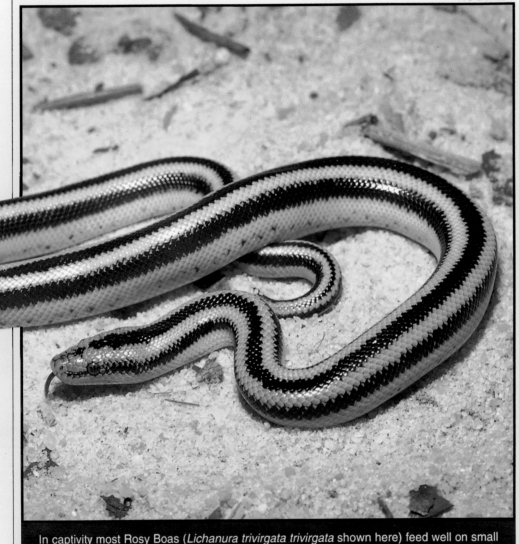

In captivity most Rosy Boas (*Lichanura trivirgata trivirgata* shown here) feed well on small mice, adults often preferring fuzzies or half-growns. Most Rosys adapt well to frozen and completely thawed food, making them easy to maintain.

Rosy Boas, especially captive-breds, are good mouse-eaters. Young snakes take pinkies, while full-grown Rosys will take adult mice. A pinkie or two every week will do for babies, with one mouse every ten days or so for adults. Most Rosy Boas will take frozen and thawed mice. Because Rosys are active mostly at night or at least during the dusk and dawn period, food should be provided in the evening.

BREEDING

Though the Rosy Boa comes from near-desert areas with hot summer temperatures, the winters often are quite cool. To ensure successful breeding, Rosy Boas must be overwintered for about three months at a lower temperature. Starting about November, the temperature should be slowly dropped and feeding reduced. By December the temperature should be down to about

55°F (13°C). Hold the snake at that temperature until March or so (at least 12 weeks is the preferred time for overwintering) and then bring it out gradually to normal terrarium temperatures and feed heavily. You want females, especially, to gain considerable weight before breeding. Sexes should be kept separately.

In April a male can be introduced into the cage of a female. Mating should follow shortly and continue over the next week or so. After you are sure the female has been fertilized, return the male to his cage and increase the available heat in the female's cage to about 86°F (30°C) with warmer basking areas. Like other ground boas, pregnant female Rosys like it warm. They often also do not eat much or at all during the pregnancy.

Birth should occur about September. An average litter consists of five or six young each about a foot long, but up to 13 young are recorded in a litter. The young are feisty but do not really bite. There are instances where the mother has eaten her young, so each baby should be removed shortly after birth and put in its own terrarium.

Most captive-bred young will take pinkies as soon as they complete their first shed (two days to two weeks), and there even are reports of young taking food before their first shed. However, like most other ground boas, some young will refuse to feed. This seems to be normal. Remember that they were born just a few weeks before the temperature starts dropping in nature, and probably many young would not

This obviously gravid female Mexican Rosy Boa, *Lichanura trivirgata trivirgata*, will like to stay a bit warmer than normal. Give her a larger heating pad and perhaps more heat in the way of a hot rock or better basking area.

K. H. SWITAK

begin to feed before it is time to go into the winter "hibernation" period. Many keepers thus overwinter non-feeding young much as they would an adult. If the young are feeding well, however, it might be best to maintain them at normal temperatures over their first winter and not tax their strength or slow their growth.

Young Rosy Boas grow fast and are mostly grown by their second winter. Maturity normally takes about three or four years, but the snakes can live over 15 years. Females tend to breed every two years in nature, but this often is not true in captivity.

TAXONOMY

Traditionally the Rosy Boa has been divided into three subspecies, and most of the herpetological literature still follows this division. The Mexican Rosy Boa, *Lichanura trivirgata trivirgata*, has three bright deep chocolate brown, even-edged stripes running from the head to the tail against a creamy to bright khaki background. The stripe over the middle of the back is about the same width and intensity as the stripes on the lower sides. The belly is creamy white and almost unmarked. This subspecies ranges from extreme southern Arizona and Sonora, Mexico, over the southern half of Baja California.

Facing page: Mexican Rosy Boas, *Lichanura trivirgata trivirgata*, are attractive, easy to keep little boas that have gained quite a following in the last decade or so. Captive-bred specimens are relatively inexpensive and good buys. Photo by I. Francais.

The Desert Rosy Boa, *Lichanura trivirgata gracia*, was considered to be a quite variable form found from western Arizona through much of southern California. In many ways it looked like a Mexican Rosy, with three rather even stripes above against a pale background lacking darker spotting. However, the color of the stripes tended to be paler, often some shade of orangish brown, tan, or even rosy brown and the belly often had many brown flecks.

The Coastal Rosy Boa, *Lichanura trivirgata roseofusca*, was considered to be the subspecies of southwestern California and much of northern Baja California. It was defined by having the dorsal stripes pale, often grayish brown, and poorly defined against an often grayish or bluish brown background color. The stripes had irregular edges and there usually were many spots of dark color in the pale background. The belly might be pinkish in some specimens.

An additional subspecies, *Lichanura trivirgata bostici*, was described from Isla Cedros and Isla Natividad in the Gulf of California, essentially a Mexican Rosy with subtle differences in scalation.

Because Rosy Boas were not that common in collections, the exact ranges of these subspecies were uncertain and there were large areas from which only a few specimens were available. Until the 1960's there even was little evidence that the subspecies actually intergraded (traded genes, intermated) where their ranges came into contact.

In the late 1980's the accepted taxonomy was challenged. More specimens from throughout the range of the species were available, many being kept alive by hobbyists. Enthusiasts who had kept large numbers of Rosys realized that there

was more variation in the species than could be described by three subspecies and also that some of the odder and more interesting color patterns seemed to be restricted to only small parts of the range of the species. This led to a review of the genus by David Spiteri, who has recently described two new subspecies, recognized an old synonym, and decided that the subspecies *Lichanura trivirgata gracia* and *L. t. bostici* are not valid.

Because Spiteri's conclusions have been published in literature accessible to hobbyists and not in the mainline herpetological journals, much of his work has been ignored by professional herpetologists but widely accepted by hobbyists. I frankly have no idea if Spiteri's work will hold up and eventually be accepted, but it seems likely that his names and concepts will hold in the hobby for awhile. Thus it is important that the Rosy Boa

More typical of the Rosy Boas that occur in the United States is *Lichanura trivirgata myriolepis* (formerly *L. t. gracia*) of southern California. Notice the uneven stripe edges and the numerous small spots between the stripes. Photo by K. Lucas.

enthusiast know the "latest" names and be able to know what to expect if something is ordered by name only. The synopsis below mostly follows the article by Spiteri in *The Vivarium*, 5(3), Nov.-Dec. 1993, and centers on color characters as all details of scalation differences have not yet been published.

It might be best to follow the subspecies from south to north. Three subspecies occur in Baja California, one of which also extends through western Sonora, Mexico, into southern Arizona. Two of these subspecies are strongly striped. The Mexican Rosy Boa still is *Lichanura trivirgata trivirgata* and still is defined by having bright chocolate or liver brown stripes with even edges over a pale creamy background. This is the form of the southern half of Baja (Baja California Sur), Sonora, and southern Arizona (including *L. t. bostici* as a synonym). The central portion of Baja is inhabited by a similar but even more strikingly colored subspecies, the Mid-Baja Rosy Boa, *Lichanura trivirgata saslowi*. This strictly Mexican subspecies has even-edged dorsal stripes that vary from dark brown to deep cinnamon, making some specimens among the most colorful of the Rosy Boas. Often the scales low on the sides have blackish edges. The eye color varies from orange to gray, and it has been suggested that more than one subspecies or type might be recognized within *saslowi*.

Ranging along the northwestern coast of Baja north to the California state line is a form that tends to have the stripes so irregularly edged and with so many spots in the often obscured dark bluish gray to brown background that it has been termed the "unicolored" phase by some hobbyists. According to Spiteri this is the true *Lichanura trivirgata roseofusca*, originally so named because of a specimen with a pinkish belly. The common name for this form now would stand as the Baja Rosy Boa, though I suspect that most hobbyists would be more comfortable with the name Unicolored Rosy Boa.

The Desert Rosy Boa of southern California into adjacent southwestern Arizona is considered by Spiteri to represent a distinctive

K. H. SWITAK

Though described somewhat by accident, it appears that the name *Lichanura trivirgata arizonae* is valid for the Arizona Rosy Boa. This subspecies is much like the Desert Rosy Boa but has more even stripes, among other differences.

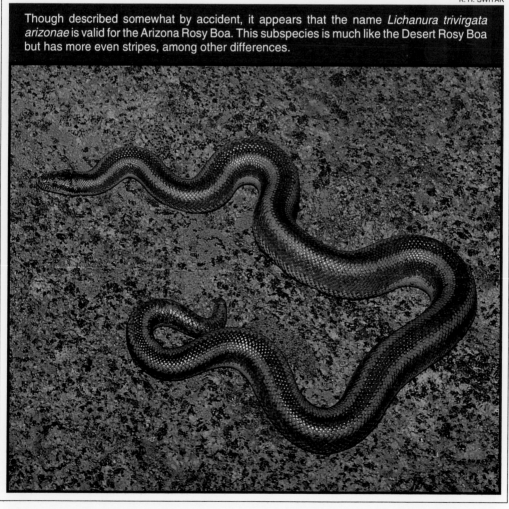

R. D. BARTLETT

The even-edged usually orangish or bright tan stripes of *Lichanura trivirgata saslowi*, the Mid-Baja Rosy Boa, make it one of the more attractive and popular subspecies.

subspecies for which the old name *Lichanura trivirgata myriolepis* is available, *L. t. gracia* being a synonym. This is the common form where the stripes are irregularly edged and the background usually has many small spots or blotches the same color as the stripes. This subspecies is very variable but usually can be distinguished by the spots in the background color.

Spiteri believes that the Rosy Boa of western central Arizona differs sufficiently from the Desert Rosy Boa to be considered a distinct subspecies, which he (more or less accidentally) named *Lichanura trivirgata arizonae*, the Arizona Rosy Boa. (Though his publication was not intended to be the formal description of the name, distinctions are given and the name has to be considered validly proposed.) This Arizona subspecies has even-edged brown stripes over the back plus a supposedly very constant belly pattern consisting of two brown dots on each ventral scale and a single dot on each subcaudal scale, all forming regular rows. Whether herpetologists will accept this subspecies remains to be seen.

I know this brief summary of subspecies may be confusing to some readers, but I'm sure that when you start looking closely at specimens in

R. D. BARTLETT

A very attractive specimen of *Lichanura trivirgata myriolepis*, the Desert Rosy Boa. This is an extremely variable subspecies.

the pet shops and comparing them you will see just how variable this species really is. I've given you the names and at least some of the characters...whether you wish to use them or not is up to you.

Unless you have trouble keeping the humidity levels down, a nice captive-bred Rosy Boa, regardless of the subspecies, may be the perfect introduction to the ground boas: readily available, pretty, easy to keep, and not all that expensive. Give one a try.

Facing Page: Top: A young specimen of the Desert Rosy Boa, *Lichanura trivirgata myriolepis*. Photo by K. H. Switak.
Bottom: Heating only a particular section of your boa's enclosure by way of an underground heating device is a sensible way of providing warmth. By leaving another section cool, you give the snake a choice. Photo courtesy of Hagen.

R. D. BARTLETT

Though most specimens of the Mexican Rosy Boa, *Lichanura trivirgata trivirgata*, on the market are captive-bred, many still are imported wild-caught specimens. Fortunately, this is quite an adaptable snake.

Facing Page: Most Rosy Boas from southern California have been captive-bred because California laws prohibit the sale of native herps. This *Lichanura trivirgata myriolepis* shows the typical irregular stripes of the subspecies. Photo by I. Francais.

SAND-BOAS

The sand-boas of the genus *Eryx* are close relatives of *Lichanura* and *Charina* but occur only in the Old World, ranging from southern Europe through central Asia and over much of Africa and the Middle East. At least ten species seem to be valid, many with several poorly defined subspecies, and there also are one or two rather questionable species names floating about in the literature. A basic list of better-known species, with suggested common names, follows:

•*Eryx colubrinus*, Kenyan Sand-Boa

•*Eryx (Gongylophis) conicus*, Rough-scaled Sand-Boa

•*Eryx elegans*, Elegant Sand-Boa
•*Eryx jaculus*, Javelin Sand-Boa
•*Eryx jayakari*, Arabian Sand-Boa
•*Eryx johni*, Brown Sand-Boa
•*Eryx miliaris*, Central Asian Sand-Boa
•*Eryx muelleri*, African Sand-Boa
•*Eryx somalicus*, Somali Sand-Boa

Facing page: Because the Desert Rosy Boa, *Lichanura trivirgata myriolepis*, of southern California is such a variable snake, it often is difficult to identify photographs. Both the snakes shown here probably belong to the same subspecies, but the snake below is the color of many *L. t. saslowi*. Top photo by R. D. Bartlett. Bottom photo by B. Christie.

S. MINTON

A juvenile Brown Sand-Boa, *Eryx johni*, is fairly typical of the sand-boas though not as colorful as many other species.

•*Eryx tataricus*, Tartar Sand-Boa.

Most of these species have been kept in captivity at some time or other, but currently only four or five species are at all common in the hobby. Each differs somewhat in their terrarium requirements and breeding biology, but basically their care is similar to that of the Rosy Boa.

Sand-boas are rather small (under 3 feet with few exceptions), very stout-bodied boas with blunt heads and short tails that resemble each other in shape and often color. The scales are small and non-overlapping, and in many species the scales over the vent and on the tail are weakly to strongly keeled. One species, the Rough-scaled Sand-Boa, has all the body scales keeled or with a conical projection and has a pointed tail; it differs enough from the other *Eryx* in its skeletal structure that is has been put into its own genus or subgenus, *Gongylophis*. In all the sand-boas the eyes are small, have vertical pupils, and often are shifted toward the top of the head, allowing the snake to burrow and leave only the top of the head exposed.

As a rule the sand-boas are nocturnally active burrowers found in

B. KAHL

Adult Brown Sand-Boas, *Eryx johni*, have a very simple pattern and often are just plain brown. If you look closely you will notice traces of the juvenile black bands on the tail. Though some Brown Sand-Boas are bright, almost iridescent brown, most are relatively unattractive snakes.

dry habitats, usually savannahs but sometimes deserts with shifting sands. They like a dry terrarium with a substrate layer deep enough to allow continuous burrowing. Many keepers like to use fine sand, while others like corncob mulch and similar uniform media. Provide a depth of at least 3 inches and preferably 6 inches so the boa can feel comfortable. Maintain temperatures in the upper 70's F by using an undertank heating pad or cables plus a rock with a basking light over it. The temperature usually is allowed to drop a bit a night, so you are supplying a cycle of temperatures ranging from 77 to 95°F (25 to 35°C) during the day down to 68°F (20°C) at night. A water bowl should be supplied and kept fresh. Actually, many keepers report that their sand-boas never drink, but why take chances if it doesn't hurt? Decorations are not really necessary, though some sand-boas will climb and even bask on low branches. The hideboxes should be low and partially buried in the sand to make the snake feel most at home.

Most sand-boas are quite gregarious, so several can be kept in a single 20-gallon terrarium if they belong to one of the smaller species. In fact, mating success may be increased by allowing several males

K. H. SWITAK

One of the more common sand-boas in the hobby is the Rough-scaled Sand-Boa, *Eryx conicus*. This species has one of the most attractive patterns of any species commonly seen on the market, is easy to keep, and is less likely to disappear into the bottom of the terrarium than are other sand-boas.

to compete for the attentions of a breeding female. To better control feeding, however, it might be best to house the boas separately so you can see exactly which snake is feeding well and which is not.

Unlike some of the other ground boas, sand-boas usually feed well in captivity, preferring a diet of pinkies, fuzzies, and subadult mice. Most specimens can be trained to take frozen and completely thawed food. Just remember that the boas are nocturnal and feed best at night, so offer the food in the evening when the lights go out. Males are unlikely to feed during the breeding season, which is very stressful for them and probably prevents them from living as long as females, though pregnant females also may not feed for several months. Probably these boas are adapted to survive for long periods during harsh winters and summers (depending on species).

Males usually have larger spurs than the females, and use them to cause the female to raise her tail to allow copulation. Males actively search for females at night, following scent trails laid by the females. Mating often occurs while the snakes are partially buried in the sand, the entwined heads and fronts of the

R. T. ZAPPALORTI

The Rough-scaled Sand-Boa, *Eryx conicus*, is an exceptionally stout species with a very short tail even by sand-boa standards.

J. MERLI

During mating, the male Rough-scaled Sand-Boa lifts the tail of the female enough to insert a hemipenis into her cloaca.

bodies below ground while the rears of the bodies project above the sand. I'll mention more specifics about breeding cycles and litter sizes with the species discussions. All the sand-boas of course give birth to fully developed young.

ROUGH-SCALED SAND-BOAS

One of the most common sand-boas, *Eryx conicus,* also is the most unusual in many respects. As mentioned, it differs structurally from the other *Eryx* and is recognizable on sight by the presence of keels, often conical in shape, over all the body scales and even those of the head. Unlike most other sand-boas, the tail is pointed, though still quite short. Males have obvious though small spurs near the vent, while in females the spurs are very small and partially buried under the scales, virtually invisible. At about 2 feet in total length, it is easy to keep two males and a female in a 20-gallon terrarium with a substrate of sand, corncob, or even plain mulch. Like the other sand-boas it even can be kept on newspaper and paper towels if given hideboxes, but somehow it doesn't look as nice on such an artificial background.

This is one of the prettiest of the boas and has a quite consistent pattern though it occupies a fairly large range over much of India and adjacent countries, where it prefers dry savannahs. The background usually is a pale bright sandy tan to grayish tan, and there are three rows of deep red-brown blotches with blackish edges over the back. All three rows of blotches tend to fuse into irregular and often broken stripes, the midback stripe being

R. T. ZAPPALORTI

Supposedly in India the Rough-scaled Sand-Boa, *Eryx conicus* (below), is confused by the peasants with the deadly Russell's Viper, *Vipera russelli* (above). Frankly, I don't see much similarity between the two snakes, but a hysterical snake-hater may not look that closely.

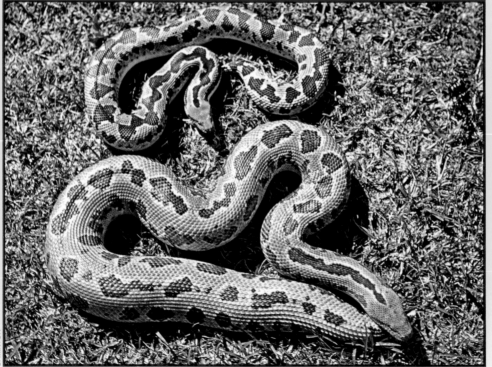

S. MINTON

especially wide and often appearing to be made up of large diamonds. The stripes on the lower sides are less conspicuous and more likely to be extremely irregular. The belly and lower sides are creamy and may be spotted. There is a certain resemblance between the Rough-scale and the deadly Russell's Viper (*Vipera russelli*), one of the most feared Indian snakes, but whether this is mimicry or just coincidence is uncertain. The sand-boas are harmless and seldom bite.

As a rule, Rough-scales mate in the spring in the Northern Hemisphere. Males often are kept cooler than usual (down to the upper 60's F) for a month or two before mating season, but this is not necessary. Females breed every two years in nature but this is not always the case in captivity. When mating occurs in March or April, birth follows in about July or August, but none of this is written in stone. Females like to keep warm, so remove a mated female to a separate cage (or remove the males) and increase the area of the undertank heating pad and give her more warm spots. Do not expect pregnant females to feed well until after delivery.

Litters usually consist of six to ten young, but up to 17 young have been recorded. The young typically molt after two or three days, when they can be given their first meal of pinkies. Sexual maturity may take two to four years, and lifespans of 10 to 15 years are not uncommon.

ASIAN SAND-BOAS

Three or four other Asian sand-boas are fairly available to hobbyists and even have been bred on occasion. They can be kept much like

R. D. BARTLETT

A newly born Brown Sand-Boa, *Eryx johni*, can be a very attractive snake. Specimens from the western part of the range often retain at least portions of the juvenile pattern, but eastern adults tend to be plain brown.

Rough-scaled Sand-Boas, *Eryx conicus*, are quite variable in details of the color pattern and general coloration but are hard to confuse with any other *Eryx*. Juveniles (bottom) may be brighter overall but do not differ much in pattern from adults (top). Notice how every scale has at least a small pimple in the center, often becoming heavy rough keels in adults. Sand-boas have a mixture of small, irregular scales and larger more normal plates on the head, the details varying with the species. Top photo by F. J. Dodd. Bottom photo by P. J. Stafford.

the Rough-scaled Sand-Boa, including a similar spring-summer mating and delivery cycle.

The Brown Sand-Boa, *Eryx johni*, is a large species for the group, sometimes exceeding 3 feet in length. When born it is pale tan or even creamy gray and has narrow, widely spaced dark brown dorsal blotches over the body and tail. Over most of the range these blotches gradually fade as the background color darkens, resulting in a uniformly shiny brown boa with only vague traces of bands on the tail. In the western part of the range, however, the bands never disappear completely, so even adults are fully banded. The tail of this species is very blunt and ends in a rounded scale.

Mating usually occurs in April or May and birth in August or September. The young are quite large by sand-boa standards, often 9 inches long. They are slower to molt than typical *Eryx* and may not take their first meal until almost two weeks old. Like other sand-boas, they usually take a pinkie or two

each week until a few months old, when they can be switched to fuzzies. Adults take subadult mice, often one every 10 days. Unfortunately this species is not often available to the average hobbyist and its rather dull coloration works against it, but it does make an excellent pet.

The Javelin Sand-Boa, *Eryx jaculus*, is known by many other common names, especially Spotted Sand-Boa. It is common over a wide range from southeastern Europe (Greece and the Balkans) through Turkey and the Middle East north into Armenia and the cold Asian steppes. Though several subspecies are recognized, they are difficult for the hobbyist to distinguish and probably best ignored unless you are trying to breed pure lines. The coloration of the Javelin Sand-Boa is not impressive, unfortunately, which has helped limit its popularity. Over a dull orange-tan background is a pattern of brown blotches that have very irregular edges and often fuse to produce a network of brown with orangish spots. The blotches low on the sides often are very small spots that may or may not fuse with the larger blotches of the back. Spurs are present in both sexes and fairly conspicuous.

Average specimens are only 12 to 18 inches long, making them very easy to house. Javelins are easy boas to keep and do well even when crowded, but give them room and they will do better. A daytime temperature of 86°F (30°C) works well, as does a sand substrate several inches deep. Commercial breeders have emphasized that seasonal changes in photoperiod (hours of light per day) and temperature are best for successful breeding, but individual hobbyists with a few pairs seldom have bothered with such details. For all practical purposes the Javelin Sand-Boa can be kept much like the Rough-scale. Five to ten young about 5 inches long comprise a typical litter, which is born in the late summer or fall. Give each young boa

Young Brown Sand-Boas, *Eryx johni*, are large by *Eryx* standards and grow into adults that may exceed a yard in length. Unfortunately, few specimens on the market retain the interesting pattern of this subadult. Photo by J. Wines.

C. BANKS

Javelin or Spotted Sand-Boas, *Eryx jaculus*, are very variable snakes. Though several subspecies have been described, they are hard to distinguish even with the use of scale counts and the color patterns overlap considerably. These two specimens give an idea of the amount of variation in the species.

S. MINTON

its own cage and feed on pinkies.

Because this species has suffered considerably from over-collecting and also from land development (not to mention human politics) over much of its range, purchase only captive-bred specimens of the Javelin Sand-Boa. This odd little boa makes a good pet, but I have to admit that its subdued color pattern never will aid its popularity.

Both species have subdued patterns of darker brown spots or blotches on tan or gray and are not especially attractive. Like the other Asian species, they tend to mate in the spring and give birth in later summer or fall. Their young are small, usually 5 to 6 inches long, and number about 10 to 20 per litter. Though good pets, they have little more to offer than their rarity on the market.

P. FREED

This female Javelin Sand-Boa, *Eryx jaculus*, is typical of the species in general color pattern and shape. Notice the very short, stubby tail typical of all the sand-boas.

Much less common in the hobby are the Tartar Sand-Boa, *Eryx tataricus*, and the Central Asian Sand-Boa, *Eryx miliaris*. Both are species of the colder steppes of Asia, so they need a cool period of a few weeks at perhaps 60°F (16°C) to breed most successfully. The Tartar Sand-Boa is a large species often almost 3 feet in length, while the Central Asian Sand-Boa is a bit smaller, seldom more than 30 inches.

KENYAN SAND-BOAS

Eryx colubrinus is a very typical sand-boa in shape and size (reaching about 24 to 30 inches in total length), one of three common African species that prefer dry savannahs across the continent. However, it is the only African species that is found in the terrarium hobby with regularity. In the pet shops it is represented by the lovely *Eryx colubrinus loveridgei*, originally imported from Kenya and

S. MINTON

S. KOCHETOV

The species of sand-boas usually are identified by herpetologists by looking at details of the head scales and making counts of the various rows of scales on the body and belly. Because the species are so variable, it often is difficult to identify photographs. The two snakes at the top probably are the Tartar Sand-Boa, *Eryx tataricus*, while that below is the Central Asian Sand-Boa, *Eryx miliaris*, but it would be hard to single-out identifying characters.

S. KOCHETOV

P. J. STAFFORD

One of the prettier sand-boas is the Kenyan, *Eryx colubrinus*, especially the subspecies *loveridgei*. Sometimes the yellow background assumes a bright orange tint.

Tanzania but now widely bred in captivity. The species actually occurs over much of eastern Africa from Egypt south and also over most of the Middle East. The Kenyan subspecies differs visibly from the rest of the species only in the intensity of its coloration, bright orange blotches separating irregular black blotches over the back, with smaller black spots on the lower sides. Often the whole pattern gives the impression of orange chain links on black. In this subspecies the colors are very contrasting and specimens often are iridescent, appearing to be lacquered. These are gentle little snakes that are easy to keep, mostly nocturnal, like it warm and dry, and feed well on pinkie mice to subadult mice depending on age and size.

Unlike the Asian sand-boas, the Kenyan has a slightly different breeding cycle. Mating occurs in the Northern Hemisphere during the heat of the summer, usually June and July, with birth following about four months later in late fall, October or November. Using two or three males may lead to more competition for the female and better success with larger litters. Mating couples may remain completely under the sand except for their vents and tails projecting up through the sand. As usual, pregnant females like it warm, so give them added heating. The young are fairly large, about 8 inches long, and number the usual 10 to 20 per litter. Females probably breed every two years in the wild but may be fertile every year in captivity.

The Kenyan Sand-Boa usually is the most readily available sand-boa in the pet shops, though most specimens probably still are wild-caught. However, there are some captive-bred pets out there if you look hard enough. Either this species or the Rough-scaled Sand-Boa should make an excellent introduction to the world of small burrowing boas.

PACIFIC ISLAND GROUND-BOAS

Scientists and hobbyists alike have a fascination for animals that are "misplaced" in relation to other members of their group. Would anyone really go out of their way to get a Fiji iguana (*Brachylophus*), spending thousands of dollars and becoming international criminals (these are really protected animals and people have gone to prison over them) if it occurred in Panama along with the Common Iguana? Until their import was strongly restricted, Madagascan boas (*Acrantophis* and *Sanzinia*) headed the want lists of many boa hobbyists although these genera are barely separable—if separable at all—from *Boa* and *Corallus*. With the species of *Candoia*, the Pacific island ground-boas, we have a similar case of popular misplaced animals with a certain mystique.

Three species of *Candoia* are found over much of the great southern Asian island arc from the Celebes (Sulawesi) and eastern Indonesia through New Guinea and the Solomons east to Fiji and Palau, including many large and small islands in this gigantic range. Each of the three species in the genus is extremely well-defined and distinctive, enough that I wouldn't be surprised if eventually they were placed in separate genera. They are the only boas that co-exist with pythons (there seem to be no pythons in Madagascar with the Madagascan boas) yet they show virtually no similarities to pythons that cannot be explained by adaptations to similar climates and foods. *Candoia* is closely related, at least according to most studies, to the slender boas, *Epicrates*, of tropical America and the West Indies.

It is assumed that their ancestor reached the Pacific islands by a pregnant female rafting from South America, a rather strange idea that really is hard to accept considering how long these boas must have been isolated from South American ancestors. Curiously, rafting—an animal being trapped on a log or mat of vegetation that sets off to sea to eventually land on another shore—seems to be an acceptable idea to most scientists for the origin of these very distinctive and specialized boas, yet the Madagascan boas—which are barely distinct from South American boas—are considered to be ancient relics of a once more prominent Old World boa fauna.

Any way, all three species of Pacific island ground-boas appear on the market in some numbers, though only one species, *Candoia carinata*, is actually common. In this genus we have a real problem with common names, as there seems to be absolutely no logic or consistency to the names used in the literature and by hobbyists. For this reason I would like to propose the following common names, some of which are familiar, some not:

Candoia aspera, Short-tailed Ground-Boa

Candoia bibroni, Round-snouted Ground-Boa

Candoia carinata, Square-snouted Ground-Boa.

These names are based on physical characters that can be seen in captive specimens without regard to island names, which generally are meaningless to hobbyists to begin with. I'll use these names here, but you can use them or not as you prefer.

SQUARE-SNOUTED GROUND-BOA

Like all the species of *Candoia*, *C. carinata* has strongly keeled scales and a broad, sharp-edged rostral scale at the tip of the snout. The common name refers to the obvious head shape caused by the prominent angular fold or ridge from the eye to the snout (the canthus rostralis) that when combined with the broad rostral scale gives the whole face a distinctive look. Positive identification can be made by glancing at the scales around the eye. In this species the supralabials, the upper lip scales, go up to directly touch the lower edge of the eye. In the other two species of the genus there is a row of small scales, the suboculars or lorilabials, separating the lip scales from the eye. The tail is long and very prehensile in this species, which is at home both on the ground and in low trees and shrubs.

I won't attempt to describe the color pattern of this species other than to say it generally consists of dark gray or brown blotches completely or partially joined by a dark zig-zag band down the middle of the back on a gray to bright reddish background. There are indications that the many described patterns (I've noted at least eight different pattern descriptions in the literature) are genetic but not restricted to any particular localities. Young from a single clutch often have two or three different patterns that may change as they grow. Once you've seen any of the patterns you should have no problem identifying this boa.

R. D. BARTLETT

The only really common Pacific island ground-boa is *Candoia carinata*, usually imported from the Solomons. Though the usual form with the zig-zag stripe down the middle of the back often is called subspecies *paulsoni*, there is no scientific basis for using this name in the hobby as it is a synonym of *carinata*.

W. P. MARA

The color and pattern of the Square-snouted Ground-Boa, *Candoia carinata*, are exceedingly variable and perhaps at least partially under genetic control. Notice the long, straight-edged snout typical of this species and distinctive among the boas.

Though commonly called the Solomons Ground-Boa (or some variant thereof), this species actually is quite wide-ranging and common from eastern Indonesia through the entire New Guinea area and then over the Solomons group. There are some indications that two types (less than species and not subspecies) of Square-snouts exist, one relatively long-tailed, the other shorter tailed as indicated by counts of scales under the tail, with most specimens from New Guinea being long-tailed and those from the Solomons and outlying regions being short-tailed.

Commonly a subspecies is recognized in this form, *Candoia carinata paulsoni* from the Solomons. However, it has been demonstrated rather conclusively that this name no longer should be used because there are no features that can define the form. Supposedly *paulsoni*, which is the type most commonly seen in the hobby, has the back pattern consisting of a dark zig-zag band joining the blotches of the midback and has the blotches on the lower sides weak or absent. This pattern may occur anywhere, though it is most common in specimens from Santa Isabel and Choiseul, Solomons. At these localities more than one pattern occurs, including snakes with distinct blotches over the midback and the lower sides and without a connecting line. Other differences such as scale counts are too variable to be meaningful when compared to variation over the entire range of the species.

The Square-snouted Ground-Boa is a rather small species, usually less than 4 feet in length in large females. Males are about 20% shorter than females, on average, and more slender. Big females may be very stout, but always appear more slender than the Short-tailed Ground-Boa. Sexes are easy to distinguish by examining the area of the vent for spurs. In this species only males have spurs, which are quite long (as much as a fifth of an inch) and heavy. Females of the Square-snout seem to always (expect some exceptions) lack spurs. If you insist on probing, males allow the probe to go about a dozen scale rows down, while females stop the probe after just three or four rows.

Keeping the Square-snouted Ground-Boa is relatively simple and they are a hardy species if they eat. The terrarium should be roomy (a 20-gallon terrarium is fine) with a substrate that is not too dry but definitely not wet. Everything from corncob mulch through orchid bark to peat moss has been used and recommended by some keepers. An interesting aside is the recommendation that peat moss is the best substrate because this snake often "worries" its prey for awhile on the ground and may pick up lots of debris, which is swallowed with the food. Peat moss is harmless when swallowed accidentally, while various mulches may cause intestinal problems. Other keepers feel there is no problem with the usual mulch substrates.

These snakes do well at temperatures in the upper 70's to low 80's (say, 75 to 86°F, 24 to 30°C) and can be kept at warm room temperatures if given a basking rock with heat bulb and a pad heater under the tank. As usual, try to confine undertank heating to half or less of the cage so the snake can retreat to a cooler corner when necessary. Square-snouts seem to be active at all hours of the day and night but seem to prefer to feed at night. The temperature does not have

W. P. MARA

The top of the head in the Square-snouted Ground-Boa is covered with irregular scales and the eyes are placed well to the side of the head. The rostral scale is very broad and sharp-edged.

to drop significantly at night, but it does no harm if the pad heater is turned off for a few hours each evening. No special lighting is needed, though the usual combination of a daylight fluorescent and a special broad-spectrum reptile bulb will do no harm.

Decorations should consist of suitable low hideboxes into which the snake can wedge itself. A high hidebox should not be used because it forces the snake to burrow into the substrate to retreat. Remember, snakes like the feel of a solid object against their sides and back when they are relaxing. Many Square-snouts like to climb, and do it very well, so provide sturdy, well-anchored climbing branches. Be sure the cage lid locks on securely to prevent escapes. This snake can feed while hanging by its tail, so obviously it can reach areas of the cage that you might not expect.

Feeding *Candoia* boas may be a problem if you cannot get nice captive-bred stock. In nature the Square-snout feeds both on the ground and in the shrubs, taking a variety of prey. When young it feeds largely on lizards, especially small skinks, plus the occasional frog. As it gets larger it switches to mostly small rodents, including various Asian rats and mice. Occasionally birds and larger mammals might be taken, but this is exceptional. Though many specimens quickly adapt to frozen and thawed mice (pinkies for young, fuzzies or subadults for larger specimens) given once every week to ten days, many do not. These non-feeders may need to be given living or frozen and thawed lizards or at least mice that have been scented with lizard blood or broken tails. In captivity these difficult feeders have taken feeder geckos and anoles, and I assume that for hobbyists in the southern United States they would feed on Ground Skinks, *Scincella laterale*, usually an abundant and easily collected little skink.

Square-snouts, like the other Pacific island ground-boas, seldom are bred in captivity. They have proved difficult to consistently produce, possibly because of differences in the biology of specimens from different localities that are imported and mixed at random in the hobby. As a general rule, mating occurs in the spring or

This view of the Square-snouted Ground-Boa, *Candoia carinata,* shows two important identification characters: the absence of a row of small scales under the eye and the prominent ridge or canthus rostralis running from the eye to the nostril.

W. P. MARA

early summer of the Northern Hemisphere, usually April through June. Many keepers recommend cooling males a bit (down to the low 70's F) for a couple of weeks before breeding season, but others never cool either sex. One male can be used for several females and there is little or no male-male fighting, which makes housing breeding pairs easy. As a general rule, separate the sexes for several weeks (perhaps over the entire winter would be best) before mixing them for mating. For some reason taking the female to the male is recommended, but this makes little biological sense and it would be better in theory to put a male in with a female that has already covered her cage with her sexual scents. The male uses the spurs to cause the female to raise her tail so his hemipenis can be inserted. Copulation may take an hour or two, rarely longer. Paired snakes that show sexual activity can be kept together for a month or longer to assure high fertility of the eggs. They do not fight, at least not seriously.

A pregnant female likes it warm. Once she is alone in her cage, give her an extra basking area and increase the undertank heating temperature and area. You'll find she spends much of her time basking now and may not eat much. Birth occurs some four to six months after mating, with liters of 10 to 20 young (with highs well over 60 young) commonly from November through January. At this point your problems really begin, because baby Square-snouts are very small, only 7 to 9 inches in total length, and have slender heads. They have their first molt within one to two days of birth (sometimes as long as a week, however) and then need food. Some may immediately take pinkies, but others may require small lizards or

lizard tails at first. Some will not feed at all and may never come around. It seems that babies can go a long time before taking their first meal, so do not give up hope; keep trying various combinations until you have success. If you annoy the young too much they react by going stiff and pretending to be dead. Females seem to breed only every two years, though there is some conflict about this in the literature.

Expect the usual problems when you purchase a wild-collected adult or half-grown Square-snouted Ground-Boa. The snake will be stressed from capture and shipping and commonly is suffering from high parasite loads. A trip to your veterinarian with your new pet would be a wise move, at least for a basic worming treatment. With good care a specimen of this boa that feeds well should give you many years of pleasure and possibly some young.

SHORT-TAILED GROUND-BOA

This very short-tailed, heavy-bodied ground boa has gained some fame of late among hobbyists for its resemblance to the Death Adder, *Acanthophis antarcticus*, with which it sometimes is found. For this reason it recently has acquired the common names of Viperine Ground-Boa and Mimic Ground-Boa. The pattern usually consists of larger blotches down the middle of the back and smaller blotches on the lower sides, often reddish brown or dark gray against a muddy cream to grayish background. When the blotches fuse across the back into complete bands the resemblance to a Death Adder is heightened. However, over much of its range it does not occur with the Death Adder and does not have the color pattern modified to look like a Death Adder, so mimicry, if it occurs, is limited to only small areas of the

P. FREED

In some parts of its range, the Short-tailed Ground-Boa, *Candoia aspera*, bears a strong resemblance to the Death Adder, *Acanthophis antarcticus* (below), one of the most dangerous elapids. Whether this is mimicry or just coincidence is hard to prove. The boa does not always occur with the adder and even where the two occur together their patterns are not always similar.

M. PANZELLA

The extremely short tail and very stout build easily allow the Short-tailed Ground-Boa, *Candoia aspera*, to be identified. Most specimens in the shops are wild-caught imports, and this species seldom is successfully bred—so far.

B. KAHL

range, especially the vicinity of Lae.

The most obvious feature of the species is the extremely short tail, which is less than twice the length of the head and may have as few as 11 rows of scales under the tail. The tail is so short it is not really prehensile and cannot even form a complete circle, unlike the longer, freely flexible tails of the other two species of the genus. The eye is separated from the upper lip scales by a row of small scales, while the snout is relatively rounded. The Short-tail is restricted to New Guinea and adjacent islands, where it occurs at low altitudes.

Apparently this boa cannot climb and does all its hunting on the ground. Though common, it is poorly understood and not often collected for the hobby market. When disturbed it may roll into a ball with the head at the center, much like several small burrowers. Most of its feeding occurs at night near water, and in some areas it seems to prefer frogs to other prey, though stomach content studies indicate that small specimens feed heavily on skinks like the other species of *Candoia*, while adults feed on small rodents. Few specimens exceed 3 feet in length.

Almost all specimens of the Short-tail seen in the hobby are wild-collected, and there are few records of successful breeding. It can be kept much like the Square-snout, though it tolerates a higher humidity (perhaps to 80% or so). Pregnant wild-caught females have given birth in the winter, so assumedly it breeds much like the Square-snout. Females often have small spurs. This strange species definitely deserves more attention from hobbyists.

ROUND-SNOUTED GROUND-BOA

Candoia bibroni is a long (to at least 6 or 7 feet in big females), slender, very arboreal boa with a strongly prehensile tail. Found from the Solomons east to Fiji and the Samoas (and rarely in eastern New Guinea), this big species has a distinctly rounded snout and a row of scales separating the eye from the upper lip scales. The color pattern is about as variable as in the Square-snout, ranging from blotches to stripes and even unicolored tan specimens. Like the other members of its genus, it feeds largely on skinks when young and on rodents when adult. Of course it needs a higher cage with adequate climbing branches to be comfortable in captivity.

This species seldom has been bred in captivity, the few specimens you are likely to see in the shops being wild-caught. It would seem that its breeding cycle is a bit different from the other species, with mating occurring in the fall and birth happening in the spring in the Northern Hemisphere. The young are not especially small but still are hard to start feeding. This is not considered to be an easy species in captivity, but if you think of it as a rather strange slender boa, *Epicrates*, you might have better success than if you think of it as a relative of the Square-snouted Ground-Boa, which

Candoia bibroni, the Round-snouted Ground-Boa, is a large, arboreal snake that is a ground boa only by relationship, not by its habits. Notice that the canthus rostralis is absent between the eye and nostril and that there is a row of small scales under the eye.

R. D. BARTLETT

is quite different. Most females have spurs, so probing may be necessary.

If you want to try a Pacific island ground-boa, start with the Square-snout, which is the most obtainable and inexpensive of the group as well as the most adaptable. More hobbyists should try to breed this species (as well as the other *Candoia*, of course) before all the forests disappear from the Solomons and the other Pacific islands that the boas call home. You cannot expect that wild-collected specimens will be on the market in numbers for many more years.

A. V.D. NIEUWENHUIZEN

Wild-caught specimens of the Burrowing Python, *Calabaria reinhardti*, of western Africa are not uncommon in the shops and on dealer lists. The species is easy to keep but hard to breed.

THREE "PSEUDO-BOAS"

I'll admit right at the start that including these three species of small burrowers in a book on ground boas is a stretch. Two traditionally have been considered pythons and the other a member of a separate family, and all three lay eggs. Actually, I need them to make this manuscript come out to a decent length, they are kept just like Rosy Boas, most hobbyists don't care about taxonomy at all, and there is no reasonable way to include these three oddballs in any other small book, so you, dear reader, are stuck with them.

BURROWING PYTHONS

Calabaria reinhardti is a strange West African snake often called the African Burrowing Python or Calabar Burrowing Python. I'm shortening the name to Burrowing Python for convenience (and does anyone still remember where Calabar was?), but that doesn't change the fact that this is one of the most poorly known of the pythons. Traditionally it has been considered a python derived directly from the genus *Python* and probably from the Ball Python, *P. regius*. Like the Ball Python, the Burrowing Python rolls into a tight ball when disturbed, putting the head at the center of the ball. However, other herpetologists on reviewing in detail the anatomy of the Burrowing Python feel it might actually be related to the Rosy Boa and Rubber Boa. Perhaps next year someone will suggest it is related to something totally different, so who knows?

Regardless, the Burrowing Python is an interesting snake though not an exciting one. Adults are about 3 feet in length, rather stout in form, with a compact, rounded head and a short, rounded tail. This is one of the "two-headed" snakes that uses the short tail as a diversion when attacked, holding the tail up and hiding the head. From a distance, and sometimes even at first glance in the hand, the head and tail can be confused unless you look for the eyes and check the scale patterns. The head scales are variably fused and fragmented in a quite irregular way, but the rostral scale is wide, with a long projection back between the internasals, a condition typical of burrowing snakes in many different groups. The color pattern is unusual, consisting of vague dark brown blotches on a paler brown to yellowish brown background, the entire snake being so irregularly patterned that often it appears to be clay-colored with darker brown dappling and paler brown spots. Generally the head and the tail are darker, sometimes almost black. Juveniles tend to be darker than adults and more evenly colored. Healthy specimens are solid-looking and somewhat iridescent.

West Africa is a warm, humid region, and the Burrowing Python prefers similar terrarium conditions. It also is an extreme burrower. For a 20-gallon terrarium with a vented lid, provide a substrate of sphagnum (peat) moss, coarse sand, and potting soil or something similar at least 3 to 6 inches deep and top it with another inch of good quality mulch. An undertank heater near the center or one end of the terrarium should provide sufficient heat when accompanied by a flat rock with a basking light in one corner. This snake sometimes is active during the day and will occasionally bask. A water bowl and a tight hidebox along with a few other hiding places should complete the decorations. If you want to provide lights, a white fluorescent combined with a good reptile-spectrum fluorescent should cover all the requirements. After you see if your specimen is active or not, you might want to try a few hardy plants or some nice plastic plants, though expect them to be tipped over every few days. There are repeated reports in the literature that some Burrowing Pythons like to climb and are quite good at it, so a few sturdy climbing branches might not be a bad idea. Do not let them get too close to the lid, however; remember how strong a burrowing snake can be.

Misting the terrarium every two days or so should sufficiently increase the humidity. Be sure the top inch of the substrate is moist, but not wet. You might want to think of the bottom of the tank as two areas, one more moist, one drier, misting half more than the other until you determine which level your specimen prefers. Burrowing Pythons often do not come from rainforest habitats but instead from savannah edges. Such imported specimens might like it drier, much like a Rosy Boa tank.

As far as I can tell, all Burrowing Pythons are wild-caught imports, with all the problems implicit in that statement. Expect your specimen to be stressed from crowded holding and shipping containers, so once you get it into the terrarium, give it a few days to adjust with minimal disturbance. A visit to your veterinarian wouldn't hurt, as you can expect it to have high levels of intestinal parasites that should be detected and treated by a

R. D. BARTLETT

Imports of Neotropical Pythons, *Loxocemus bicolor*, seem to be timed to the presence of young snakes. Most of the specimens available in the hobby are half-grown young. Notice the projecting "hognosed" snout.

professional. Unfortunately, most pet shop specimens are rather inexpensive animals and many keepers do not want to spend the time and money on competent vets, thus many pets die within a few months of being purchased.

Feeding may be a problem at first, but an adjusted Burrowing Python should take fuzzy mice. As commonly is seen in burrowing snakes, the mice either are constricted or more commonly are pinned to the walls of the burrow by a loose coil until inactive. This is one of those snakes that may never adapt to frozen and thawed mice, but it is worth the effort to see if you can get a specimen that is feeding well on live fuzzies to make the transition to frozen food. It has been reported that recent imports may prefer lizards as food, something to consider when all else fails.

Breeding in captivity so far has been a complete failure with this species. Occasionally gravid females are imported and successfully lay eggs, but so far few or none have hatched. In nature it seems that mating occurs in November or December, with eggs being laid about five or six months later, in April to June. The clutches typically consist of three or four very large (4 inches long and over 1.5 inches in diameter) elongated eggs. All attempts at incubating the eggs in captivity have failed because the eggs are very sensitive to fungal and bacterial infections and always go bad after a few weeks. A few matings in captivity have been noted, though usually they have produced only infertile eggs. The male's spurs are a bit larger than the female's but the sexes are difficult to distinguish without probing. In adult males a probe will extend for about ten subcaudal scale rows, while only extending a maximum of three or four in the female. Considering the large size of the eggs and their delicate nature, the possibility should be considered that in nature the female incubates the eggs and controls the temperature and humidity of the clutch.

The Burrowing Python is an excellent pet for the hobbyist who has tried the simple boas and pythons and is looking for a challenge. So little is really known about the best conditions for keeping this species that there is much room for experimentation, and the possibility of breeding this odd species in captivity is virtually untouched. Next time you see a *Calabaria* in the pet shop, rescue it to a nice terrarium and give it a chance.

NEOTROPICAL PYTHONS

The concept of a python existing in the New World is difficult for most herpetologists to accept, but there is little doubt that *Loxocemus bicolor*, the Mexican Burrowing Python, Dwarf Python, American Python, etc., has the skull of a python, an otherwise strictly Old World group. However, it also has many features of the skeleton and soft anatomy that indicate it is related to the sunbeam snakes, Xenopeltidae, so it often has been put in its own family, Loxocemidae. I'm going to ignore its family status and also shorten its common name a bit to the more appropriate Neotropical Python because it is found not only in southern Mexico but through much of northern Central America. It has been collected on the Pacific slope from Nayarit, Mexico, south to Costa Rica and on the Atlantic slope from Chiapas, Mexico, south to Honduras.

An even better name for this species might be the Hognosed Python, because of its unique head shape. This snake is a burrower, and like many other unrelated burrowers

R. D. BARTLETT

The Common Sunbeam Snake, *Xenopeltis unicolor*, can be one of the most iridescent of the snakes in the proper lighting, a quality hard to capture on film. This is one of the easiest to keep of the truly "oddball" snakes but it seldom is bred, unfortunately.

it has a large, upturned, rather bluntly pointed snout much like that of a hognosed snake (*Heterodon*). The eye is large and the snake is fast to recognize movement. At some 4.3 feet in maximum length this is not exactly a small snake, but most specimens that reach the hobby are much smaller, 2 to 3 feet in length, and possibly immature. The head and body are a solid dark brown to nearly black with a bluish to reddish iridescence, while the belly varies from uniformly cream to uniformly gray. In fact, once two species of *Loxocemus* were recognized based on belly color, the name *sumichrasti* being applied to dark-bellied specimens. Further research and many more specimens (this species once was considered to be very rare

but now is known to just be hard to collect) showed that both belly colors occur in the same populations and seemingly only one species is represented. Often the dark color of the back is relieved by small white or creamy spots that may merge into larger pale blotches.

In nature the Neotropical Python is a lowland species that seldom penetrates far into the foothills. Typically it is found in rather dry forests and near-desert situations, but it also has been collected in lowland forests with rather high humidities. In the terrarium it does well with several inches of good mulch on the bottom of the cage, a water bowl that is kept fresh, several hiding places and a hidebox, plus a basking rock to keep the temperature a few degrees above room temperature, dropping a bit at night. This species does not need especially high temperatures and, being active almost only at night, does not need special lighting arrangements. It will climb if given a few branches, however.

Hobbyists who have kept *Loxocemus* report that it is a hardy snake that takes small mice and chicks well in the terrarium. As with other wild-caught burrowers, it might be necessary to feed living fuzzies and pinkies at first before trying to move the snake on to frozen and thawed food.

The sexes look much alike and are, as usual, best distinguished by probing. Female scent glands allow probe penetration to only three scales, while male hemipenial pouches may let the probe extend for over a dozen scales. Eggs appear to be laid in March and April in nature, with hatchlings emerging by May and June. Wild-caught females sometimes lay in captivity, but matings in the terrarium are rare. The eggs have proved hard to incubate, but limited success at about 86°F (30°C) has been reported. Clutches are small, usually about four eggs.

The Neotropical Python is not a common snake in the terrarium hobby, but it is sometimes collected as young specimens and exported in small numbers. If healthy, these adapt well to captivity and can be long-lived pets. As usual with wild-caught snakes, it is best to have a competent veterinarian give your new pet a careful exam for parasites before you bring it home. Keep the terrarium dark for at least the first few weeks until the snake adjusts, and make sure it is drinking. Again, this is an interesting snake but not an especially exciting one for the average hobbyist.

SUNBEAM SNAKES

One of the most widely distributed snakes of Southeast Asia is the Common Sunbeam Snake, *Xenopeltis unicolor*, a placid burrower found from southern China and Burma south into Indonesia, the Philippines, Borneo, and the Celebes. For many years this was the only species of sunbeam snake known, and it still is the only one available to hobbyists. In 1972, however, a second species, the Hainan Sunbeam Snake, *X. hainanensis*, was described from eastern China. Although much like the Common Sunbeam in appearance, it differs in several obvious characters of head scales and appears to be a good species that should be looked for in recent imports from China.

Basically, the Common Sunbeam is a rather small (3 feet or less), heavy-bodied snake with a rounded snout and very short tail. It lacks the spurs of the pythons and boas and at first glance looks much like a "normal" snake, being related to both the Neotropical Python on one side and the pipesnakes (*Cylindrophis*, etc.) on the other. It is chocolate brown above, paler on the belly, the scales of the sides and belly usually outlined with white. Often there appear to be several darker stripes along the back, but this usually is the result of the brilliant, multicolored iridescence that is this snake's major attraction. Technically, *X. unicolor* (the Common Sunbeam) has two postocular scales behind the eye, eight upper lip scales (labials), and 35 to 45 teeth on the maxillary bone. The Hainan Sunbeam (*X. hainanensis*) should have a single postocular scale, only seven upper lip scales, and 22 to 24 maxillary teeth, as well as fewer ventral scales (152-157 vs. 164-196) and subcaudals (16-18 vs. 22-31) than the Common Sunbeam.

The Common Sunbeam is considered by many to be one of the most innocuous snakes. It never bites and seldom even makes false biting moves. The mouth is rather small and the jaw bones are not especially flexible, so its prey is limited in size. In nature it feeds on snakes, frogs, and lizards as well as the occasional nestling rodent and bird, and in the terrarium it takes all these foods readily. It seems to adapt well to frozen and thawed pinkies and fuzzies, making it an easy snake to care for.

The terrarium can be very simple, a few inches of mulch on the bottom, some hiding places, a bowl of water, and a basking area. High heat and humidity are not necessary, though it wouldn't hurt to have an undertank heater to keep the temperature closer to 80°F (27°C) than 70°F (21°C). Spray the tank every two or three days to keep the top layer of substrate moist but not wet. Special lighting is not needed and this snake seldom basks. In nature it is nocturnal or crepuscular (active at twilight and dawn), but in captivity it does not seem to be disturbed by light and even has been kept on a newspaper substrate with limited hiding places. However, a dark terrarium should be less stressful than a brightly lighted one and thus preferable.

Until recently the Common Sunbeam Snake was available commonly and inexpensively as wild-caught specimens from Thailand and other southern Asian localities. It seldom was bred in captivity because the supply seemed endless, but recently several countries have placed restrictions on collecting this species and it has been seen less and less in the hobby. Whether the Hainan Sunbeam will be imported to replace it is uncertain but could happen considering the present economics of many Asian countries. Fortunately, however, it can be bred in captivity, laying clutches of 6 to at least 15 eggs. The sexes are difficult to distinguish (remember that the tail is extremely short, less than 10% of the total length, in both sexes) externally, and it may be necessary to "pop" the hemipenis of the male if probing does not distinguish the sexes. Little has been reported on mating behavior, but assumedly it occurs in the evening. Incubation at about 84°F (29°C) has been recommended. The hatchlings are beautiful little iridescent snakes with distinctive white collars on the neck that disappear with growth. They feed better on small frogs and lizards than on pinkies but can be raised if given sufficient care.

Their iridescence makes Common Sunbeam Snakes one of the most unusual snakes that can be kept easily in the terrarium, and they certainly are worth purchasing next time you see one in the pet shop or on a dealer's list. Remember, they may become difficult to obtain in the near future. Also, the possibility of running into a species unreported in the terrarium literature, the Hainan Sunbeam, should make the heart of the serious hobbyist flutter with excitement. These are pretty, interesting, fairly easy snakes that have been neglected in the past and deserve more attention before it is too late.

SUGGESTED READING

TW-128, 592 pgs, 1400+ color photos

TS-144, 208 pgs, 200+ photos & illus.

TS-194, 192 pgs, 175+ photos

TS-193, 736 pgs, 1400+ color photos

TS-189, 224 pgs, 180+ color photos

KW-127, 96 pgs, 80 color photos

TW-111, 256 pgs, 180+ color photos

AP-925, 160 pgs, 120 photos